Rose-Colored Glasses

Rose-Colored Glasses

A Memoir of
Love, Loss, and Hope

Jo Ann Simon

E. L. Marker
Salt Lake City

published by E. L. Marker, an imprint of
WiDō Publishing
Salt Lake City, Utah
widopublishing.com

Starfish icon taken from Seashell pattern background created by Natkacheva—Freepik.com
Summer beach vintage pattern seamless vector from FreeDesignFile.com
Eiffel Tower @ Trocadéro photo by GuilhemVellut—Flickr.com

Cover design by Steven Novak
Book design by Marny K. Parkin

ISBN 978-1-947966-04-8

Printed in the United States of America

FOR TOM

Thank you for everything, my love

Crescent Beach, Block Island, Rhode Island

He felt bad that I went,
I felt bad
we both felt bad together making
it something good.
Something called love.

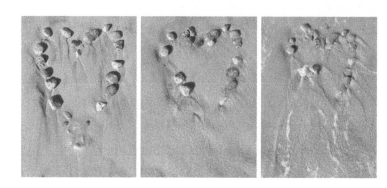

Contents

Dear Tom,

I need your help.

I have been invited to go to Block Island for Labor Day weekend with Blondie and Martin, along with an entire cast of supporting characters.

I don't know if I can do it.

I don't know if I can ever go back to our beloved Block Island without you.

I don't know if I have the strength.

Will you be my chivalrous knight in shining armor, who always came to my aid gallantly, no matter why or where I needed you? Can you be there for me on Block Island somehow?

I ache with missing you. I wish that you could be here to give me a big, reassuring bear hug of encouragement like no one else can. I always felt your strength penetrating my being when you told me that I can do anything that I set my mind to. When I had your arms wrapped around me, with my head crooked under your chin, feeling so secure and strong, I was capable of anything. You helped me find my confidence.

How can I do this? I need your arms around me, tied into a bow with a double knot that will stay strong to bolster me up. Then, I can try to live this new life alone.

There is an inner strength inside my core that helped us through our living and your dying, but I just don't know that I can wear those rose-colored glasses anymore.

Love always, Me

Chapter One
2014
Block Island Weekend

I could not fathom why no one had posted signs.

FOR LABOR DAY WEEKEND, I RETURNED TO BLOCK
Island, Rhode Island where it all began three years ago. It
had been one hundred and three days since Tom died, and
I still could not believe he was gone from this earth. Or that
he would not be walking down that beach with me.

I love this ferry ride, approaching the island with a bird's
eye view of the artisan clay cliffs, standing strong and tall
above the unending beaches and waves. It's like they are
there to hold up a piece of sublime heaven for our wishes
and dreams to come true. But there would be no enjoyment or intimate champagne celebrations like in the past.
This would be different.

I had to go on deck to feel the island wrap its arms
around me with a sultry lick of salt air. I heard the musical
cries from the seagulls swooping down to find food. With
tiny goose bumps on my arms, I shivered with trepidation,
despite the sun casting the last warm rays of summer.

Block Island features seventeen miles of pristine
beaches, protected by lighthouses and spectacular bluffs

and surrounded by rolling roads and winding paths. Many of the beaches encompassing the island are isolated and nearly untouched, providing breathtaking views and utmost tranquility. The island is located twelve miles off the Rhode Island mainland.

As I stepped off the ferry, I felt the same Block Island energy I had felt with Tom that cataclysmic weekend. But it was not the same. Nothing would ever be the same again. The beauty of the sea, the boats, stately buildings that had withstood the countless storms would never have the same magic for me. I wanted to have a positive frame of mind, but that clammy gray veil of misery hovered over me, casting a shadow of anguish.

Blondie and I have been friends since high school. She, Martin and I walked up the hill while I attempted unsuccessfully to talk sense into myself.

"Blondie, where are the signs? Do you see them?" I asked. I expected to see signs that said: *Warning! Protect yourself from ticks on this island. Lives have been lost!*

There were no signs.

"No, I don't see any. Maybe they're at the beach?"

After all Tom and I had been through, I could not fathom why no one had posted signs. Then I realized it had been my responsibility to inform the island officials. I should have told them a tick bite from Block Island had led to my husband's death. I should have, but I did not. I was too involved in trying to save his life.

Blondie knew this would be a tough trip for me. It was wonderful that all my friends were coming to support me and try to help me out of my downward spiral. Blondie is a wonderful lifelong friend who is always there for me. Her effervescent smile and personality always helps to cheer anyone up. Martin, her husband, always has a smile and a song on his lips, with that special Irish gleam in his eyes.

"Jo Ann, it will be okay. Don't worry about the signs for now," Martin said.

Blondie added, "Let's just enjoy the beauty and not worry. We brought bug spray for protection, and we can warn people, too."

When I agreed to join my friends on this weekend, I made a pact with myself to come here, where it all started, to face my demons. To try to move on with my life. I did not realize how the brutal force of reality would hit me between the eyes, like a crowbar prying open my brain and delivering the facts front and center like a reality show of "This was your life!"

Everything I had tried desperately to file away in the dark archives of my brain came flooding back. The memories came in cascades of sadness, desperation, and hopelessness, carving out a piece of my heart. But the flashbacks also showered me with amazing thoughts of how we loved each other through it all.

I tried to not cry. I tried to be normal, but it was okay. Everyone who knew me was used to my crying, and I didn't care what strangers thought.

I looked around in the crowd of vacationers coming off the ferry and realized I was looking for Tom. He would have stood out with his six-foot linebacker size. And with the brightest colored polo shirt and wildest plaid shorts, worn with his classic Dockers boat shoes that took him everywhere. One would wonder what mischievous thoughts were under those dark sunglasses. You just knew he was fun to be with. I half-expected him to randomly show up.

Back to reality . . . I was ready for whatever this weekend would deliver. Those memories I had tried desperately to hide could come back. I would face and savor them during these four days on Block Island, and beyond. I pulled the strength together to open those magical doors and recall the wonderment of our short life together, and how we both had hope despite the doom hovering over us.

Especially, I needed to remember the tender moments we shared every single day, and how he made me the happiest person in the world, no matter what was happening to his body, his person, his life.

I hoped I could find some peace here.

Chapter Two
2014
Stone Hearts

Sitting there by myself on the edge of my world . . .

I COULD NOT WAIT TO GO THE BEACH TO RELIVE my time with Tom here.

My eyes popped open with the first light of day, before the alarm went off. I could not imagine rolling over back to sleep. The hotel was quiet as a church, with only a rooster crowing in the distance.

Martin and Blondie had a room upstairs. Mine was on the ground floor, right by the front door overlooking the porch. I tried to book the same room where Tom and I had stayed, but since it was not available, I took the room next door, almost identical to "our" room. It gave me a calming courage to relish the memories of past times that crowded the empty space.

I quickly brushed my teeth, washed my face, dressed, and put a hat on my crazy hair. As I stepped onto the wooden porch, I stopped for a moment to savor the scene. Overflowing, vibrant, floral hanging baskets danced in the breeze coming off the ocean, scenting the crisp air.

I felt relieved that no one had showed up to join me for a walk on the beach. I couldn't imagine being with anyone but Tom on this walk.

As I walked through town that morning, the sun was a beacon trying to cut through the fuzzy morning haze. It was mesmerizing. A couple of sleepy dog walkers moved in quiet slow motion while the sound of the surf in the distance bid me a salty "Good Morning." I wished it was a good morning. I could not help but wish that the clock could be rewound to recast our destiny. *How am I going to get through this weekend?*

I passed the landmark Surf Hotel and entered the beach access right after the Blue Dory, with a golden lab bidding me hello with his bark. As I stepped onto the sand barefoot, a sensation of calm touched me, with a massage of tiny granules erasing my worries. The beach always calmed my soul.

I started my long walk on Crescent Beach toward the spot where he and I sat three years ago. I could remember how he had held my hand and picked up special shells for me. He had skipped rocks over the water with his boyish, show-off charm.

There was an outcropping of rocks to cross over, no problem with the low tide. I walked the long stretch and felt somewhat at peace, being there with the fresh soothing breeze, the smell of the ocean and the sunshine on my face, knowing I was not alone. I felt Tom's energy all around me and it felt incredible. Being here now was the right thing for healing, no matter how painful to remember what I had lost. The waves echoed my thoughts with thunderous, powerful repetitions of beauty.

I reached the spot and sat down on the sand, closed my eyes, remembering.

I could almost hear the buzz of people around us that day, three years earlier, laughing and talking quietly, respecting everyone's space. I remembered the children with their energetic enthusiasm, building sand castles, running back and forth to get water to fill the moat around their castle. They had brought me back to my own childhood, playing on the beach with no cares whatsoever.

It had been a very hot day, that day, but a cool refreshing breeze had been coming off the surf as it rolled in, making it feel like drinking an icy, crisp gin and tonic while sitting next to a stoked pizza oven. The beach walkers ranged from middle-aged men and women with I Don't Care paunches and leathered skin to the young and hip, strutting their stuff with lots of cleavage and booty.

Our merry foursome—Susan, Doug, Tom and I—had set up on the edge of it all, relaxing with our rum and Cokes, sunscreen, and great company. Tom was doing his crossword puzzle, as only Tom could. He had an affinity for crosswords, especially in the *New York Times*. He would start on one corner and work his way through the entire block systematically and quickly. I was amazed at how fast he could accomplish that feat when I couldn't even get the first five on the list. I considered myself smart, always an A student, but I definitely flunked crosswords, compared to Tom the genius.

Of course, I had other smarts that he did not, why we complemented each other so well. It still astonishes me that I didn't want anything to do with him when we first met, and now he is my everything.

Susan and Doug were blending into the landscape with that inevitable comfort level that only best friends share. Susan is beautiful inside and out. She has the biggest heart and an insatiable love of fun and work. We met through work and clicked immediately. We are always asked if we are sisters. We both have round faces with short pixie hair and big brown eyes. My hair has been painted silver from chemo and life, which is how people tell us apart. We will always be there for each other in times of joy and sadness as sister best friends forever are.

Doug is the perfect mate for Susan. Like us, they complement each other. Doug and Tom shared a special bond as only boys can do with nonstop talk of sports and life in general. I was inhaling every last shred of it, thinking we were the luckiest people in the world. Memories . . .

I sat for a long time, crying, wondering for the hundredth time why I had agreed to come here to relive such precious moments with him that I will never have again. Tom wanted me to live my life for him and for me. He told me he would not be happy if I stayed home and wilted away, mourning him. We were both extreme people-persons who loved to socialize and enjoy the world around us. It was daunting to try by myself to jump back into the social life that we had, but I would try, one step at a time. This weekend was a big first step.

Sitting there by myself on the edge of my world helped me think clearly. I needed to figure out how I could live again. I felt as if my entire persona had changed, and that I was also dying. I was not sure who I was, or who I wanted to be. I knew I was a widow, but that label didn't seem appropriate for me. I remained very in love and connected to Tom even though he was no longer on this earth, but I also knew that he wanted me to go on and live my life to the fullest. This is a lot easier said than done. Maybe not even possible.

I thought, the best I can do is stick my toe in the water and check the temperature; to see if I should come back another day or just sit on the edge with my feet in the water, watching the scene from the sidelines. For too many years, I was a sit-on-the-sidelines girl, but the past three years had changed me to a dive-in girl. I had decided that life is too short to wait for the right temperature while I miss out on the thrill of just plunging into that water.

So, I picked myself up with a new resolve and headed back to the hotel, back to Blondie and Martin. There had been a storm the day before, and the waves were huge and magnificent as the tide came rolling in. When I approached the rocks, the water was almost to my knees. I tip-toed slowly, trying to hold my balance against the playful waves, but they took me down onto the rocks. I laughed hard; it felt good to laugh out loud. I knew that Tom was laughing, too, and we were both smiling together.

After I picked myself up and shook off the water, I kept going slowly and made it to the other side of the rocks. I took four steps and then I saw it—a flat rock sticking up in the sand. When the waves surrounded the water and receded, a perfect three-foot heart formed again, again, and again. It was as if a paintbrush had come down from heaven and mixed the sand, water and a dose of love to create a masterpiece watercolor in the sand. I knew it was Tom's message of love for me. It was mesmerizing and end-less. He was with me then and always would be.

That image would never be erased from my mind and my soul.

Upon my return, we spent the rest of the day with friends, traversing the small universe of the Old Harbor coast while eating, drinking and shopping, with panoramic views of the ocean and beach at every turn. I tried my best to keep up and appear to be having a good time. Other friends, and friends of friends, arrived by boat, ferry or plane as the day went on. As tradition would have it, everyone met up at the National Hotel with the best bird's eye view of the marina, the ocean and beaches.

Sitting there at the bar with my eyes closed, I could hear the rustling of the twelve American flags lining the front of the building. The flags saluted everyone who climbed the forty steps to the welcoming haven of the vast open-air café porch and bar. I heard the familiar clamor of knives and forks as guests enjoyed a delightful meal, clinking glasses in celebration of living life to the fullest. The aroma of fried clams and burgers with sautéed onions wafted by, but the overwhelming scent was that of the seaside. It calmed my soul.

I opened my eyes to see my circle of friends there with Blondie and Martin to enjoy the Block Island experience. I knew they were also there to help me learn to live again. I felt cozy and safe in the tightly sewn patchwork quilt of love and friendship draped around me.

My best friends, Susan and Doug, were there. When I first saw them, despite trying to contain my emotions, I turned into a huge puddle with buckets of tears, emotional despair and sadness. I snuck out the back door to try and put a blanket on my tears and resolve to be strong for my friends, even if they knew I couldn't. The hurt of Tom's absence was not only mine. This sobering thought brought me back to reality.

As tradition dictates, you celebrate a special occasion with a PC "Proper Cocktail." You have a PC after a bad day at work and you need to feel better, when it's time for *Jeopardy!*, or to celebrate something or someone special.

At the National, the official PC was a Dark n' Stormy—Gosling's Dark Rum and ginger beer with lime. Tom and I learned of this drink in Key West at the Rum Bar. We always shared it with Susan and Doug at the National. It was tall, dark, and handsome with a sweet yet tart refreshing finish. "Delightful!" as Tom always said.

The toasting of Tom began with clinking the glass and saying "*Sláinte*"—Gaelic for "To your health!" It felt like Tom was there with us. Tears formed in my eyes, but my heart brimmed with love for the past memories, and the present memories, too.

Susan put her arm around me as her tears mixed with mine; Doug tried to hold it in with true manly style. And the moment held while we all remembered Tom and said a silent prayer. I was lucky and proud to have so many incredible friends. Being together in this place was the best medicine anyone could give.

Who knew that the life you loved and dreamed of forever would end without sufficient notice? I did have notice, but it was a blip on a screen. The life I loved was gone so quickly, it is still unfathomable to me.

I came to this island not wanting to remember the time of the "illness." I don't like calling it the "illness," but I hate calling it "ALS" and hate calling it "when Tom died." It just feels so negative and creepy. Instead, I call it "the times we had together."

Whether it was when we first met, when we dated, got married, when we made every minute count when he got sick or his last days on earth, it was "the times we had together." These are the times to treasure, and that makes me feel better.

The evening lasted long into the night, with live music and good conversation. It was comforting to be with friends, doing things that Tom and I would have done if he were here.

Sleep came easily with a drowsy, lovely memory of my heart in the sand.

Chapter Three
2003
The First Meeting

"Hi, my name is Tom, what's yours?"

WHEN I MEET NEW PEOPLE, THEY ALWAYS WANT to know the story of Tom and Jo Ann.

My favorite story is how we met.

I was newly divorced after twenty-five years of marriage. It's ironic that my first husband's name was Tom. The first twenty were the best, and then we started to travel different roads with different people and had developed new wants and needs. We were young and naive when we first met and married in the seventies. We waited five years to start a family, so we could enjoy life with just the two of us.

When we decided to start, we produced the perfect family of a girl and a boy. They were our pride and joy. The Simon family life focused on our kids being happy and us trying to be the best parents we could be. We both worked full-time at our jobs and at our home life, which was good. My busy life distracted me from my husband, while I kept up with the kids' softball, soccer, bowling league, Girl Scouts, Boy Scouts, being head of the Church School, and participating in the PTA.

I'm not sure when, why or how the change occurred, but our marriage fell apart. The Popsicle split into two separate parts, and we would never be one again. My kids were growing up, not needing me as much since they were becoming independent, promising individuals. Our family life started to crumble like a dry, old cookie.

We had agreed mutually to divorce, but not until it was the right time. Five years later, living as roommates, tired of not living life to the fullest, I asked for a divorce. I could not live this way anymore and needed to be someone again. It was the most amicable divorce ever, with me handling both sides *pro se* through the court. It was all over in a jiffy.

Our marriage, friendship, and life ended one day in a Danbury courtroom. There was no fanfare, but I think it felt like a failure to both of us.

I was forty-nine years old, or should I say young, with two wonderful children, one in high school and one in college who enjoyed their own lives. Jennifer, the oldest, was a typical earth child. As a little girl, she was the one always outside playing with the wind, jumping into the creeks looking for fish and fossils, climbing trees, and loving everything in nature. It was no surprise when she announced in fourth grade that she was going to be a Forest Ranger. She graduated from the University of Maine with a degree in Forestry.

Jennifer was then recruited to do an Outdoor Education program in Michigan, where she met her ideal husband, got married, had babies and lives a beautiful life. When I visit, it feels like I'm in Mayberry: a warm and fuzzy feeling. I always wondered how she became who she is, since I turned into a corporate person with a love of bling, even though I grew up camping and fishing with my dad.

Bill, our son, was the deep thinker. He had the brains in the family. If you gave him a math problem, he was the fastest gun in the east. You could see the numbers tumbling in his eyes like a slot machine, and then he would spit out the answer with razor-sharp accuracy. As a kid, he loved to have fun, ride his bike as fast as he could and never stop. He was a typical boy, liking everything boyish, always teased his sister, but he was a dreamer, too. He imagined great things and still does. Bill had many dreams which changed constantly, but I give him a lot of credit for reaching for the stars. He now has his own beautiful family and a great job as an accountant and CPA. I am so proud of him and my daughter.

Divorce was a new life for me. I was breathing fresh air for the first time in a long time. The future was not defined; I was just happy to finally be on my own. I was self-sufficient, with a good job, and had just moved into a townhouse with my son while he finished high school. I felt like I was on a giant springboard, jumping into a delicious new world of freedom and open space, to grow and expand into whoever I was meant to be.

My daily life at this point was comprised of going to work, shopping, meeting friends for a cocktail and gossip. It was nonchalant. I had been working for an electronics contract manufacturing firm for thirty years. I was hired as a gal Friday and eventually became Vice President of the company, where I still work today. My colleagues were baby boomers and hard working as well. We created a formidable group of friends and coworkers, building our company to its current successful stature. I will always appreciate the opportunity to learn, grow and become the person I am today. I like that person.

I had always enjoyed men in my life, including men friends, coworkers, boyfriends, dads, uncles, cousins and brothers. I loved my girlfriends, too, but it was different with men. They were a special part of the universe, and I appreciated how they accepted me as part of their manly fraternity. They made me feel like I was one of the boys and that it was okay to be on their turf. I could talk the talk with them and still be as girly as I wanted.

But loving a man was different. I always expected unparalleled love and strove to give the same. When that was not a reality, I started to lose my taste for men. After my divorce and some quick dating, I did not want anything to do with any man. I started to feel bitter and sad, so I stopped dating, immersed myself in my work and pondered what to do next.

The art world called my name. Art shows in town and at museums were some of my favorite places to visit. In my opinion, art makes the world a better place. I started as a self-taught "artist wannabe," devouring every art magazine I could find. The year after my divorce, I gave myself a birthday present of a six-week art class at the local parks and recreation center.

The class was extremely intimidating. I was the only new person without paints or brushes, just a notebook and pen. The learning started with actual painting. Yikes! Paints, paper and an easel were supplied while our instructor started painting a still life of autumn gourds and mums in an arrangement. I was petrified to put down that first brushstroke, but with each stroke, I felt calmer. It settled me down, creating something from nothing.

Learning by doing was the best medicine, jumping in and enjoying the process. We worked in watercolors, which I quickly learned is not the most forgiving of mediums, but the results can be stunning. This was what I needed, to realize there was more to life than sitting home feeling sorry for myself.

Six weeks turned into years of classes locally and around the world. I made friends who are still part of my life and always will be. I became an official artist, selling my work locally and abroad from my daily painting blog. I felt good about myself.

Art replaced the need for men in my life.

My clients loved my work and style, but I never thought it was good enough. My thirst for learning everything I could to improve my art became my mission in life. The Internet allowed me to explore every end of the earth to investigate art, and how I could be part of it, in order to continue my artistic growth.

An art co-op was born in the old train station in the center of town with a group of incredibly talented artists. They voted me in to be the president, not so much for my creative talent, in my opinion, but more for my business acumen.

Every six weeks, the walls would change with a new themed show. Each member was required to sit the gallery for a few hours a week. My art education included art lingo, as well as painting. I quickly learned that we would "sit" the gallery, not "sit in" the gallery. We were actually babysitting the artwork.

It was thrilling to see what wonderment came through those doors. It could be tiny or huge, abstract or photo-realist, watercolor, oil, acrylic, multimedia or some new and exciting medium. We accepted all forms of art including pottery, jewelry, subway-tile work, and even cows.

We are famous for creating the top-selling cow "Tiffany" at the Cows on Parade in New York City. It was a joint effort to paint the cow in classic Tiffany design, which was created by one of our members. It was so exciting! There was a camaraderie of the artists to share their techniques, tales and talents with each other. The vibrant feeling was contagious and inspiring.

One show was all about ballet. At the show's opening, paintings on the walls mirrored dancers performing on the floor in constant flowing movement. It was an incredible scene for the senses. One time, we had a nude self-portrait show. That brought a packed house to see who painted what.

One night after we closed the gallery, my good friend and talented artist, Deb, and I decided to go to the place across the street for something to eat and drink.

When we walked in the door at Greenwoods, we could have been in Ireland or England, with the locals talking up the day with animated, friendly fervor. There were several folks sitting at the long, weathered wood bar with its brass fittings and footrests. It was ornate as any Irish bar would be. We had been there twice before, but the only person we knew was Eric the bartender. Eric knew our drinks and served them right away.

Jokes filled the air, teasing us for the punch line. Although new to the crowd, we felt welcome and comfortable. We were sitting there minding our own business when this man showed up at our table in chef's whites and crazy, chili pepper print pants.

"Hi, my name is Tom, what's yours?"

As I soon learned, this was Tom's modus operandi. He loved people and wanted to meet everyone in the room.

Normally, everyone wanted to meet him, too, but not this night.

"I'm Jo Ann," I said politely, "and this is Deb. So, why are you dressed like this?"

He grandly spread his hands out. "I, my dear, am the Executive Chef at Steakhouse 22, at your service."

"Where is that located?" Deb asked, skeptical.

"Just over the border in New York, on Route 22."

He was likable enough, but not my type. I was not interested in the least and wanted him gone. He was six-feet tall, overweight, with these old-fashioned glasses from 1964 that should have been in the Smithsonian. His hair looked like a shag rug on steroids. I was not at all attracted to him.

Debbie invited him to sit down, to my dismay. But the conversation was engaging and entertaining, talking about food, fun and what was going on in the world, until he stopped, saying, "I am taking up too much of your time together. Jo Ann, I would love to take you out to dinner sometime soon. May I have your number?"

I was shocked. I did not expect this and could not imagine going out with him. I didn't know what to say and blurted out the first thing that came to mind. "I'm sorry, I don't have a card."

Deb, thoroughly enjoying the conversation, reached into her bag and handed over my card. I kicked her under the table, almost knocking over my cocktail. She jumped in her seat.

He grabbed that card faster than a $10,000 winning lottery ticket.

"Girls, thank you for your time, I greatly enjoyed our conversation." He looked me directly in the eye and said, "Jo Ann, I will be in touch."

Deb had always been my benevolent protector from men. She has a keen sense for good character. If we are out and a man starts a conversation, she will evaluate him in the first sentence. If she thought the guy seemed like a scumbag, she would tell him I wasn't not interested, even if I was. She had a sixth sense about who was right for me.

"Debbie, why would did you do that? I do not want to go out with him."

"I liked him. He has a good soul."

"Okay," I told her, "if you like him so much, you go out with him!"

Debbie laughed. "I can't believe I just gave him your card. It seemed the right thing to do."

"No worries, Deb. When he calls, I'll make an excuse."

He never called.

Life went on with its daily routine of work, painting at night, and working the gallery. The memory of Tom faded. Six weeks later, after we had closed the gallery, Debbie and I walked across the street to Greenwoods again and sat at the same table.

Tom walked in wearing chef whites and crazy pants. "I can't believe I finally found you," he said, coming straight toward us. "You are not going to believe what happened. I went home that night I met you so excited about taking you out to dinner. I was not thinking straight and washed my pants with your card in the pocket, which totally disintegrated. I couldn't find you. I was so upset."

My response was, "Oh well."

We did not go out to dinner anytime soon. He knew better than to ask me. He pursued me in a different way.

What I did not know on that first night is that he said to himself, his mom and his friend that he had just met the girl he would spend the rest of his life with. The first time he saw me, he knew. He had been married twice, a true romantic, but how could he know this?

He asked to meet me at the gallery while I was sitting, to see the artwork. I agreed; it was harmless, and it was good for business. He asked if he could bring lunch. Again, I agreed, to see what a chef would bring for lunch.

"Jo Ann, I hope you like the lunch I brought. I went to the deli at Carraluzzi's, which has the freshest meats in this area and Caroline just loves me, so the sandwiches are big and delish. You're half Italian and half Irish. Since you look more Italian than Irish with those deep, dark brown eyes and flawless olive skin, I thought I couldn't go wrong with an Italian combo grinder. What do you think?"

"I love it, Tom. It is delicious, but are the chips and pickles for the Irish?"

"Jo Ann, you can't have a sandwich without pickles. Chips are optional, so I guess you can call that Irish, since they are made from potatoes."

We split it. Simple, delicious, fun. Seeing Tom in normal clothes cast him in a different light, not too shabby. He was easy to talk to and interesting. Not the right guy for me, but maybe just friends?

"Jo Ann, will you join me for drinks later tonight at the pub, after you close the gallery?"

A response did not come quickly. Ignoring the question would not make it go away. I didn't want to encourage him, and it had been a long day.

"Jo Ann, it would just be time to enjoy a drink and meet some of my friends there. They might be interested in buying some of your artwork."

Smart man. "Yes, thank you."

It seemed that all eyes were on me when I walked in the door. Everyone knew Tom, and it seemed they were expecting me, too. There was a buzz of melodic harmony composed of laughter, clinking of glasses, conversations and music in the background.

Introductions started immediately at the bar with the locals, who were Tom's friends. Every intro by Tom was the same: "Hi, I would like you to meet my friend Jo Ann. She runs the art gallery across the street."

The response was almost always the same: "I've heard so much about you. It's wonderful to finally meet you."

Yes, the word had spread.

One introduction was very different. "Jo Ann, I would like you to meet my mother, Lynne." She was sitting at the bar with girl and guy friends, enjoying the evening. With short stylish hair, blue jeans and a young spirit, she did not look like she was old enough to be his mother.

"Well, hello. It is my pleasure to meet you."

Unusual meeting Tom's mom, since she did not seem like a mom at all, just one of the fascinating people at the pub. But I felt good, meeting everyone.

This pub crowd was one happy family, and it seemed that I passed the initiation and was now part of it. The camaraderie of the bar and everyone there just relaxing and being part of a comfortable space was contagious. I became a regular. But I soon learned that just being friends and enjoying the pub together was not enough for Tom.

He brought me flowers to the gallery and little notes that said I was beautiful. I didn't feel beautiful, but this made me feel like anything was possible.

After a few months, I gave him my card and cell number. He started to call me after his work, and we would talk into the wee hours about anything and everything. He kept that card proudly and prominently in his wallet to the day he died. His pursuit of me continued with increased fervor, but we did not become lovers. I still considered him only a friend.

He would tell me at every chance that I was beautiful. He even began to say he loved me. I would argue that I was not beautiful, and he didn't know me enough to love me. Self-doubt about starting a new relationship instead of just a friendship hovered like a dark cloud over my head. The debate continued in my mind about whether I was beautiful, and if he could possibly love me without knowing me.

If I had a business trip, he'd offer to drive me to the airport. When he'd pick me up, he would have fresh flowers in the visor and a cooler packed with cheese, crackers and my favorite drink: Bombay Sapphire Gin, diet tonic and two limes. He was the most thoughtful, loving person I had ever known.

I learned early on that he also had his negatives, as we all do. He was extravagant to excess. He did not have any sense of money or how to save, spend and control it. The most expensive thing on the menu was his favorite, but he would give the shirt off his back and his last dime to someone he just met who needed it. He lived for the moment and had a heart of gold.

Exceptional memory for music, recipes and sports—anything and everything about those subjects—sprang from his brain like a walking encyclopedia. Recipes were never written down; they were spewed out verbatim, on demand.

It was like having a walking, talking Google resource. Sports and music were his undeniable talent. People would call him to ask questions about music, which he would answer immediately, plus give them additional information, like date and location. Who knew when and where the Mama's & Papa's got together? And the date when they stopped playing? Tom did. It was amazing how he could retain such wealth of information but could not remember simple, everyday things.

Fashion sense was at the bottom of his totem pole. The glasses were a deal-breaker for me, if he didn't change them. He did not wear T-shirts or jeans, because he thought that a button-down shirt or polo shirt and khakis were the proper dress. I did not agree. We went shopping and changed his style. He was happy, more comfortable, and I liked the new look. He also shaved his hair down to a short buzz, which was very sexy. He could still dress in his highbrow clothes anytime he wished, but now he had a comfort zone of clothes that he enjoyed as well.

I am not a fashion plate, but I consider myself stylish and I care about how I look. I also cared about how Tom looked if he was going to be with me. Call me snobbish, but it was a great process for both of us to go through. We bonded about our looks, our feel, our vibe, and who we wanted to be.

I still thought we were just friends.

And then one night that changed. It was the night Tom literally swept me off my feet. The simple intention of the evening was to gather at my friend Soo's house for a cooking class with Chef Tom. A Caribbean menu was chosen with sous chef's Soo, Susan, Geri and me.

Soo, who is a diehard foodie, was anxious to use her new kitchen, meet Tom and learn more about his chef skills. I knew better. Girls will be girls, and these three were keenly interested in having only the best for me when it came to men. The conversation spelled out their determination.

Soo, Geri, and Susan kept egging me on that Tom was now someone special in my life. Soo, the eternal romantic, said seriously, "Jo, I think he is the one for you."

"No, no, no, he is just a good friend. It's too soon for me."

Geri, always ready with compliments, chimed in, "Jo, it's never too soon if it's right. You glow when you talk about him."

"Maybe that's from sitting in the sun too long. Being here with all of you, learning new cooking skills, is all I want right now. Let's just have fun tonight. . .no pressure."

Susan defended me. "Yeah, girls, let's give her some time . . . maybe about five minutes."

We started in the kitchen with Caribbean Bahama Mamas to kick off the cooking lessons. Then one by one, everyone dissolved into the hot tub or danced to the loud music piped through the house inside and out. I didn't want to be the last one to desert Tom, so I stayed and helped finish cooking our sumptuous meal to perfection. It had ten minutes in the oven to finish.

As if on cue, the Beatles started singing "You Really Got a Hold on Me."

"Jo Ann, may I have this dance?" Tom took my hand and guided me into the empty living room.

We didn't dance, we floated. When he took me into his arms it seemed like my feet never touched the ground. He took control with light magical moves that made my heart melt. At that moment, we became one in our own little bubble of unspoken feelings. He really had a hold on me and I didn't want this song to ever end. I could see the girls, giggling like schoolgirls, sneaking looks at us while we danced. The music ended, and he swooped me down with a dip and then a sweet kiss.

At that moment, I knew he was the one. My mind rushed with crazy thoughts. Why was I fighting him? How could I not want this feeling of strong loving arms wrapped around me, caressing my soul?

I didn't want him to ever let go of me. I knew he felt my change of heart through the electricity that pulsed between us.

Later, we enjoyed our fabulous, bountiful meal, danced on tables, sang a cappella together, friends just being friends. No one knew, except us, that true love was born that night.

Dear Tom,

   Thank you, darling, for persevering, and being the best dancer
I have ever danced with, and giving me one of the best nights of
my life.
   I love you and miss you always.

Jo Ann

Chapter Four
2004
The Love of My Life

I was afraid that if I told him I loved him . . .

TOM AND I BECAME VERY GOOD FRIENDS. HE made me feel appreciated and loved in a way I had never experienced before. It was scary at first, but then it felt beautiful, too good to be true. The best part of falling in love was being friends first. We learned everything there was to learn about each other. We shared stories of our past, from childhood to present day. We opened our secrets to each other and wept through the tough stuff, while laughing over the ludicrous. Nothing was held back.

We both agreed we never wanted to get married again. He had been married twice, me once. We wanted each other just the way we were.

He would tell me he loved me every day, and I would say it was too soon to say that and he needed to give me time and space. He did that by staying close and turning up his charm, thoughtfulness, and showing his love for me in many ways.

I especially loved his daily question: "Jo Ann, has anyone told you how beautiful you are today?"

"No, Tom."

"Well, you are the most beautiful person in the world, inside and out."

I loved hearing this and always replied, "Thank you, Tom." I wanted to compliment him, too, but still hesitated to encourage him too much.

At least once a week, he would bring flowers to my door or to my work. He would write beautiful little snippets of his love for me; or encouragement, if he knew I had something special to accomplish, like a big presentation at work or an art show.

He finally did call on Kentucky Derby day to ask me out to an official dinner date, five months after we originally met. Everything before that had been at the local bar with friends, group gatherings or just talking on the phone. It was for a pre-opening dinner that evening in town for a new Neapolitan Italian restaurant, La Zingara. Because Tom had helped the owners set up with the local purveyors, they invited him to this special event.

I was not sure I should accept. This would be considered a commitment and might make our relationship official, even though it was only a date. I was on the fence, wanting to go and try the restaurant but afraid of saying yes. Tom had not seemed like my "type"—whatever that was—but he had grown on me so much in the last few months that I really did care for him, no matter how much I was fighting it.

I felt excitement in my veins and knew in my heart the answer had to be yes. You only live once. I asked what the dress was.

Tom replied, "Casually spiffy."

He showed up in a crazy pink plaid shirt and khakis, which was adorable. Off we went to a wonderful dinner . . . and the rest is history.

His love for me was overwhelming. At first, I was choking on it. It felt excessive and something I did not deserve. I could not understand how someone could love me so innately without knowing me. And when he knew me, why would he love me? There wasn't much to love here. I did not have a very high opinion of myself and was surprised that anyone was interested in me. My failed marriage was proof that relationships were not my forte.

As time went by and we spent more time together, Tom's aura and attention gave me a feeling of something so silky and soothing that I just wanted to take a bath in it all day long. I wanted to bottle it and save it for another day. I knew it was Tom's love for me, but I also knew that it was my love for him that was growing every day.

I was afraid that if I told him I loved him, it would change everything, and what we had would never be the same. This was when I kept him to myself. I was hesitant to share him with my friends and family because of my insecurities; it was a big line to cross. Of course, everyone knew there was a Tom in my life because of the flowers on my desk, the smile on my face, my new positive attitude and outlook on life. But many of them had not met him yet.

I'm not sure why I set all these boundaries for myself and for him, but I needed to have my own space as long as possible to protect myself from being hurt or disappointed. I was on new ground, recently divorced, and was not sure that I wanted to jump into the pool without experiencing other people, places and things. Tom was the master of demonstrating that he was the only one I would ever want to spend the rest of my life with.

When I finally brought him around to meet everyone, they were quick to ask why I had not brought him sooner, and why I would question whether I liked him or not. Everyone loved Tom. He was a guy's guy and a ladies' man. He could talk turkey on sports better than anyone I know, except maybe his brother and sister. He could pull literary and music details out of his vast mental encyclopedia in a blink of an eye and then sweet-talk a girl age two or one hundred and two, to make her feel like the prettiest woman in the world.

It is interesting to me when I look back on how the evolution happened in my mind. I originally saw Tom as an overweight, old-school, unattractive man. After I got to know him, my eyes and my heart saw him as a charming, fun, intelligent, handsome, sexy, debonair man. It didn't hurt for him to get new glasses, new clothes and shave his hair to have that wonderful attractive, foreign spy look. What I saw when I looked at him was a gorgeous hunk of man. He was the one who changed the perspective for me.

What I especially loved about Tom was that twinkle in his eyes. It was very Irish, devilish and delightful, all at the same time. We could look at each other across a room and know what we were saying to each other: "I love you and want you always."

Once I decided to open myself to him, we had sex which was actually making love. It was mind-blowing, as we used to say. Hot, sensual, intense and glorious, all at once. He only wanted to please me, and I only wanted to please him. That give and take was the basis of our relationship then and all the way through our years together. That cemented our love, and the romance continued.

One day, he called me at work and asked if he could make a special dinner for me at my house. He said it was important that I call him when I was leaving and to get my appetite ready.

As I stepped through the door, I was greeted with a cavalcade of decadent scents that attacked my senses as savory, sweet and earthy. Tom came around the corner in full chefdom, with a white kitchen apron, signature blankie towel over his shoulder, and red bandana around his head. He carried two glasses of champagne, hurrying over to the stairs to block the way.

"Good evening, my love." He handed me a glass and we kissed.

"Good evening, Chef. What incredible delights will you be serving tonight?"

"Oh, the night is young, you will have to wait and see. I would like to toast to our love and to you, the love of my life."

"To us and to you, the love of my life."

It was then that I heard Andrea Bocelli playing in the background upstairs.

"I have prepared a special treat for a hardworking woman who needs to spend some time enjoying the simple things in life."

He took my hand and started to lead me up the stairs, strewn with rose petals. It was beautiful and sensual. As we stepped on the petals, the scent sprang to attention immersed with Andrea's bravado, becoming louder with each step.

We entered the bathroom, where a parade of candles cast their glow on a bubble bath strewn with rose petals awaiting me. The bottle of champagne stood on ice, ready for another pour.

My knight left me with a kiss and a whisper in my ear, "Lose the daily grind, soak up the suds and listen to what Andrea has to say. Prepare yourself for the best night of your life."

Chapter Five
2008

The Rings

The Opera Café was a huge undertaking . . .

THERE ARE MANY, MANY STORIES OF OUR EXPLOITS around the world.

Don't think we didn't have tough times together arguing about money, priorities in life and how many cats are too many, but we always were able to talk it out. His rule was that we would never go to bed mad at each other. If one of us had a problem with the other, we would talk it out. The talking might turn into yelling, but at the end it was all about hugging and kissing. Life is not easy to get through together, but it is certainly better together, especially with Tom.

I'm sure making him happy was one of the reasons I agreed to partner with him to own a restaurant. It was also exciting for me to be part of something new to call my own. My job for the last thirty years was good, but not mine to reap the benefits of ownership. This opportunity tossed our way could make both of our dreams come true, and we would do it together. We were thrilled.

The short story is that Tom and I purchased the restaurant, Greenwoods, where we first met, the same building where his mother started the first Opera Café with sandwiches and quiches back in the sixties. Tom started his culinary career learning from her, then going out on his own working at various restaurants, honing his skills. When asked where he trained, he always responded, "The School of Hard Knocks."

He eventually became an Executive Chef and famous in his own right. His dream was to own his own restaurant someday, but he never expected it would be the same place where he started his career. I became his partner, business brain, and accomplice in jumping off a bridge into unknown waters. The decision was made to name it "The Opera Café" after both his mom's first café there and the building's original purpose to house the opera.

The Opera Café was a huge undertaking, with full bar and pub, three fine-dining rooms and an outside patio in good weather. The menu was Regional Americana with my artwork depicting each region.

We had an immediate following from the crowd that was always there and knew us so well, and from new faces who loved our menu. Live music was part of our venue, and it brought folks in droves.

The town was always having festivals and activities that we were part of. We were truly a focal point in the composition of the downtown landscape. We even had a Prince and the Pauper New Year's Eve with a packed house celebration. There were two menus, one for the Prince and one for the Pauper, with everyone dressing the part. Several copies of Mark Twain's book, *The Prince and the Pauper,* were left at the bar to encourage everyone to read and be part of the festivities. Everyone was a king and a queen that night, including us.

It was grand—at the beginning.

Thank goodness I kept my day job for my sanity and protection during the two-and-a-half years of restaurant ownership. Owning a restaurant sounds romantic, fun, entertaining and elite. It is all that plus hard work, never-ending hours that blend into each other as a crazy blur, and excruciating responsibility for every little crumb, fig, staff, guest and heartbeat of the restaurant.

Then, the recession hit, which was the worst possible time to own a restaurant. People did not have expendable income anymore. They were trying to make ends meet. The first thing to go when cash is tight is dining out. As we saw our numbers erode, we tried everything in the book to attract people.

We created weekly discounted specials that were delicious but inexpensive to allow folks to join us for some relief and relaxation. Our weekly "All You Can Eat Fish Fry" became a popular meeting place and a loss leader for us. However, it seemed that nothing would work. Our overhead was too much for the current economy, and we were losing money and hanging on the threads of a tiny rope.

Invariably we squabbled about the minutiae of everyday life, to avoid talking about the giant monster looming over us. Since things were so slow, we decided it was the best time to get out of Dodge, go to somewhere sunny and bright to saturate our souls with warmth and positive energy. The Florida Keys shouted for our company.

Our exhaustion and depression accompanied the sinking of our maiden ship. Our heads were down, and our eyes were dour with the sadness of it all, but we tried to carry on the happy face to our staff and public.

It was the perfect decision. We could have been any-where, except at the restaurant, and it would have improved our mindset; but there is something so special about the Keys. It fills you with the expectation that anything is pos-sible. As you drive down that one road, soaking in the smiling sunshine with the only view of water, water, water everywhere, you know that paradise is possible.

This trip was a wise decision for us. We were able to talk everything out and make sense of what and how we should proceed.

It is easier to talk logically when you don't have the weight of the world smashing your head into the ground. We could see things in the light of day and feel somewhat optimistic that we might be able to pull this off. I wasn't convinced, but we had so much invested, we had to try. We formed a new plan and resolve with high expectations and promise. The rest of the trip was left to simply enjoy each other and the tropical haven around us.

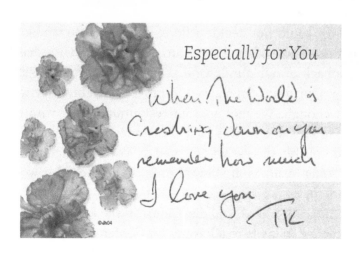

Especially for You

When the World is
Crashing down on you
remember how much
I love you
TK

Sitting at the Hog's Breath Saloon in Key West, Tom said that he had something to ask me. We had been together seven years when we went on this trip to decide how to save our restaurant.

"Jo Ann, you have made me the happiest man in the world. I have wanted to ask you this for three years now, but didn't think you would say yes, until now." He gazed into my eyes with a yearning that took my breath away. I had no idea what he was going to say. "Will you marry me?"

This was the last thing I expected him to say. I immediately started to cry. "Yes! I will marry you!"

It felt so right. We celebrated for the rest of the trip and looked forward to a long, happy, married life together. I thought Key West was the perfect place to pick out an engagement ring, but Tom wanted to pick it out himself and make it another special event in our future. I knew he did not have funds due to the restaurant situation and was content to just be engaged. In fact, I would have been happy with the prize ring out of a box of Cracker Jacks at that point.

We could not decide where, how, or when we would get married, so we settled into a normal life with that in the back of our minds while we tried to save our restaurant. Our new plan showed improvements, but they were not enough. We met another restaurant owner who was doing well, and he was kind enough to share with us what and how his success was formed. It was an intriguing way of doing business. It showed promise; we hoped it would work for us.

Since it was do-or-die time for the restaurant, we accepted an invite to a Restaurant Conference in San Francisco on this new way of doing business. It was outside the box methods, but we were willing to learn and try anything.

There were many restaurateurs there with claims of wild success using these methods. I felt like this was the last piece of straw in the barn, but it might be the one the golden egg was laid on. For three days, we worked and learned by day, and then ate our way through San Francisco by night. It was a foodie festival of delights.

We had planned an extra day after the conference to enjoy the sights and decided to calm down and ponder our future. Crossing over the Golden Gate Bridge to Sausalito is a journey for the senses. Every view is spectacular, with the jewel of San Francisco in the background, shimmering in the sunlight. The air is scented with an exotic floral salt spray scent. Calm defines the feeling.

After you cross that bridge and bear right to the tiny village of Sausalito, another feeling is defined: swanky. Everything is low-key, deliberate, well done. It lets you breathe out a sigh of relief to find a secret hideaway.

We arrived midday, to a bustling little downtown that screamed "Come See Me!" We found a parking space directly in front of a delicious line of stores to explore, and a perfect restaurant across the street with the most magnificent views of San Francisco.

Tom wanted the restaurant first, but I needed to shop. I didn't need to spend money, but I had to have the psychological medicine of shopping. Tom was not a shopper, but he acquiesced in his charming way of taking control and escorting me into the first inviting shop. Immediately, I found a funky, red-jeweled watch to add to my collection of watches in every size, shape and color. This snazzy red watch with tons of bling would bring the count to one hundred and five. The second shop had two floors with gobs of wonderment everywhere. We started upstairs, where Tom requested a private fashion show.

After several showings, the final choice was a red, white, and blue polka-dot halter dress. I'd wear it in Cleveland when we visited Mimi, Tom's grandmother, for the upcoming Fourth of July weekend visit. It matched my watch as well.

We were off to lunch when I spotted jewelry in the case downstairs while waiting to check out. I whispered, "Honey, do you see what I see?"

"What do you see, my love?"

"I see a beautiful set of wedding rings, engagement and wedding band, that is crying to be on my empty finger. I love the cut of the diamond, and the smaller diamond soldiers wrapped all around, bolstering her up. They are calling me."

He whispered in my ear, "I do see them now. They are beautiful."

I wrapped my arms around him and whispered in return, "They are only twenty-five dollars for the set, my love."

Tom sprang into action, corralling the attention of not one but two sales girls to help him. "Ladies, I would adore to have the love of my life try on those absolutely beautiful wedding rings in your case. Could you help us?"

Of course, they obliged.

Tom carried on, sharing with the gals how we met, how he knew at first sight that I would be the one he'd spent the rest of his life with. They were all gooey-eyed at the thought of it and wondering if that would ever happen to them.

They pulled the rings out of the case, and I knew which one I wanted.

Tom made a big deal out of taking it out and slipping it on my finger. It fit perfectly!

He then proceeded to get down on one knee. "Jo Ann, you have made me the happiest person in the entire world.

I love you and want to spend the rest of my life with you. Will you marry me?"

The entire store went silent, holding their breath.

I captured that moment in my heart, savored the joy of our love, waited an extra thirty seconds for the drama of it all, and said, "Tom, you are the love of my life. I will love you always. Yes, I will marry you!"

A roar of happiness and congratulations from everyone in the store filled us with a promise of better days ahead.

We almost skipped across the street, seeking a special space of our own, and champagne. We found it on the back deck with the best view of San Francisco Bay. The bay seemed especially bright, shiny and sparkly competing with the kaleidoscope from my ring.

A warm breeze helped us to nestle into each other as one. The bubbles of the champagne jumped into the competition of light. It was a brilliant moment together. We did not need to talk. We soaked up the scene with photographic memory, so we would never forget an inch of it.

There was only one couple on the far corner of the deck. The woman called over to us. "Excuse me, I just wanted to say that your ring looks absolutely gorgeous from here. It keeps gleaming in the sunshine."

"Oh, my goodness, thank you! He just proposed to me . . . he just purchased the ring across the street."

They came over to congratulate us and ordered another round of champagne to continue the celebration. They were both from Boston, here to decide whether to get married again or not. They explained that they had been together for eight years and could not decide.

Of course, we told them our story and that we never wanted to get married again either, but here we were, absolutely delighted with the prospect of sealing our lives together for good. The four of us continued our conversation of love, life and the pursuit of true happiness until it was time to go back to reality.

One last, savory, special dinner in a highly recommended restaurant in San Francisco produced Tom's wedding ring. I got out, looking for a place to get change, while Tom circled for a parking spot.

The Irish store appeared to jump out of my imagination, but no, it was real, with a green shamrock and *"Sláinte"* on the door. It bid me welcome. I entered to find an array of Irish woolens, crystal, linens, and green everywhere. When I approached the counter to make change, a lovely gal with a brogue as good as any I've heard said, "Good evenin' to ya, how can I help?"

I did not want to just ask for change, so I took a quick look around. My eyes were drawn to a case that held more Claddagh rings in one space than I had ever seen. There were silver, gold, some with stones, some with different designs; but they all bore the beguiling heart, surmounted by a crown with hands proudly holding it up.

I knew from my Irish background that these were symbolic and romantic. The heart was love, the hands friendship, and the crown loyalty. The position of the ring on the finger was intended to convey the wearer's romantic availability, or not. If the ring is worn with the heart out, it means their heart is open, and they are available for a relationship. If the ring is facing in, their heart has been captured already.

This would be the perfect wedding ring for my Irishman.

Just then, he walked in boasting that he found the best parking space, but we needed more change for the meter.

"Yes, I would love to have my fiancée try on one of your beautiful Claddagh rings."

Tom's smile lit up the room. He knew exactly which one he wanted and again, it fit perfectly. These rings spun their magic into our world.

Our last stop in San Francisco was at The Buena Vista Café, which claims the origin of the Irish Coffee. We needed to determine if it was better than Tom's famous TK Coffee. As we sipped this magical concoction, we pondered the possibilities of our future.

The verdict was that both were sensational, but TK's was the best.

After a valiant effort, we did end up closing our restaurant. It was daunting, humiliating and sad.

The turmoil of making the final decision brought us closer than we had ever been. We depended on each other for sips of strength that allowed us to hold our heads up high and focus on the future without looking back. The view through the restaurant journey had always been with those rose-colored glasses on, with positive energy and determination to be successful. Our view was ready for a change of pace.

The only good news was that now we could live our lives without the restaurant.

Our bankruptcy attorney recommended we get married immediately for tax purposes. So, on a Wednesday, we decided to get married that Saturday. The best part was that we did not have a lot to do. I shopped for a dress, Tom shopped for food.

Two of my dearest girlfriends, Blondie and Grace, thought I was absolutely mad and making a huge mistake. Since we had been the Three Musketeers through thick and thin for over fifty years, they had the right to want the absolute best for me.

I don't think their disapproval was about Tom being the right one. It was more about them not being able to attend the wedding and wanting me to be absolutely sure he was the one. I was hurt that they did not respect my decision and join in my joy, but they did not change my mind. Eventually, they realized how happy he made me and how special he was.

We were married on a small island on Candlewood Lake in Danbury, Connecticut. We were a party of five. My SBFF (sister best friend forever) Susan was the Maid of Honor and the Justice of the Peace. Her husband Doug, Tom's BFF was the best man and captain of the boat that took us to the island. My son Bill walked me down the path to give me away and was the photographer. Tom was the groom and the chef who prepared a fabulous fairy-tale wedding meal to enjoy on the island. I was the florist and the bride.

Our boat ride to Blueberry Island on a clear September day held reserved excitement, like a bottle of champagne ready to pop. The sun seemed to follow our passage to the island, spotlighting our happiness with a warm glow. There was a slight crisp breeze announcing autumn in the air. The trees were tinged with that golden change of season. We were certainly changing our season to married life. I thought, *How fitting that we will be married with this beauty surrounding us as affirmation of our intentions and love.*

Dress was island clothes with flowered shirts for the guys, bright island dresses for the gals, and flip flops for all. Susan performed the most amazing ceremony, with rose petals shaped in a heart on the sand, and fengshui candles, significant shells, unity rocks, and wonderful words:

"Fate: I've said it a few times today, because I really think that it is what this day is all about. Fate has led us here on this island on this beautiful day. I remember in the beginning of your relationship that each of you had past experiences that kept your hearts at bay. Over time, both of you let yourself love again. We all know that is not an easy thing to do for the first time, but to do it again is even harder. I don't know how many times I heard both of you say you would never get married again. Now is the perfect time to tell you both—I never believed either one of you. Those words did not match the sparkle in your eyes when you looked at each other. Those words never matched the actions you took caring for each other, nurturing each other and loving each other.

"Jo Ann and Tom, you have asked me to marry you. Do you do so as your own free act and deed? Are you willing to take that leap of faith? Then, do so now."

We stepped into the heart of rose petals in the sand as a sign of our leap of faith to each other.

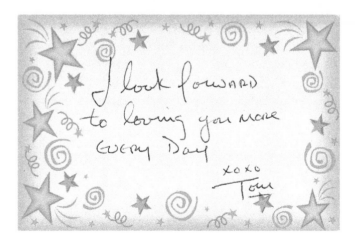

The celebration continued with an impromptu, surprise gathering of family and friends at a lakeside restaurant.

At the end of that glorious day, it was incredible to absorb the fact that we were now a married couple. When we returned home we felt exhilarated, exhausted and as content as we could be. As I undressed for bed I was not surprised to read the tags from my newly purchased wedding dress: "FOREVER."

That said it all.

Chapter Six
July 2011
The Beginning of the End

Little did we know...

IT WAS A GORGEOUS WEEKEND ON THAT FATEFUL trip to Block Island. We had been counting down the days to our favorite island getaway. We desperately needed a well-deserved separation from reality, to leave our negative vibes behind and relish the simple island life with good friends. Both the island and our friends did not disappoint, greeting us with comfort and love. My unemployed chef was ecstatic to leave behind his job-hunting, and I was always ready to escape my business world and the daily blogging about my artwork.

I remember that weekend so well. We were still in the lovey-dovey newlywed phase, even after almost a year of marital bliss and seven years of saying we would never ever get married again. I felt that there was a secret bond of Gorilla Glue that attached our hearts forever. I knew it had something to do with actually getting married and making the most sacred commitment to each other, for better or worse, through richer or poorer, no matter what or when. We were happier people, a better couple, and more enjoyable friends for it.

This weekend was ours to feast on with our best friends, Susan and Doug. Our voyage was by ferry from New London, while Susan and Doug boated from their marina on the Connecticut River.

This weekend was a chapter out of a book about the Life of Tom & Jo Ann, which was so typical of who we were and what we did in our free time. We both loved to travel near and far, Block Island being one of our favorites, enjoying fabulous food. Or hosting gourmet dinner parties for close friends. Or spending time watching sports together with pizza and beer. Or just staying home for a cozy night in front of the fire all by ourselves.

The best part was sharing the intimate details of it all with each other.

"Tom, what was your favorite food tonight?"

Tom ruminated about the question. "Oh, I loved the tuna tartare; let's try to make that at home sometime. Definitely with the spiced avocado."

"What do you think the spices were? Definitely cumin, but I'm not sure what else."

"Darling, it was curry and cumin with lime, a great combination."

As always, Tom was right.

Susan and Doug planned a special pub crawl to their favorite island spots. They wanted to show us their view of Block Island, starting at Champlin's Marina, where their boat was docked in New Harbor. We always stayed on the Old Harbor side, and were excited to enjoy new sights, tastes and adventures. You can think you have seen everything about a place and done it all, but when you look through someone else's eyes, your vision is enhanced to twenty-twenty.

Susan and Doug exude that contagious love of life tonic that acts like a magnet. Pub crawls are about eating and drinking and meeting people. Our crawl that evening was all of that, with tons of fun mixed into the fold. I could finally say that I had traveled one end of Block Island to the other, enjoying the scenery, people that we met, many laughs, songs, and our own wonderful company.

The Oar, one of our seven stops, was my favorite. The unpretentious outside of the building, sitting at the edge of a marina, did not prepare anyone for the surprise leading up the inside stairs.

The unending parade of oars in every color of the rainbow greeted us with a happy-go-lucky long oar smile. I have never seen so many oars in one place. They were everywhere—on the walls, hanging from the ceiling, without a space in between. There were big oars and little oars. Each one was personalized, some with paintings, some with writing from people all over the world.

Then there was the view! The best view of New Harbor, with the constant flow of boats of every size and shape, and gorgeous waters beyond. I could have sat at that bar forever, with that view and the buzz of camaraderie—a special place with special people.

Our last stop that night was at the Hotel Manisses, where Tom and I were staying. The Manisses, part of a group of hotels and inns, was a beautiful old building with lovely grounds, antique furniture and old-world style. It gave us a feeling of going back in time, but in a very stately, romantic way—a beautiful place to be. We had an incredible farm-to-table dinner downstairs, then capped the night with their signature ignited, flavored coffee on the patio.

Polly, our favorite resident taxi driver, picked up Doug and Susan to return them to New Harbor.

The end of the day brought warm feelings of wonderment for how lucky we were to be here, feeling like the king and queen of the world. The air was soft with the kiss of the ocean surrounding us, and the half moon, high in the sky, played "I Spy." If I could make a wish for anything in the world, it would have been this. It was as if we were in a dream.

The next day started with brunch at The 1661 Inn, the sister Inn of the Manisses.

When Tom was young, he had come to Block Island with his parents and sister, Jenny. They would call The 1661 Inn the IGGI Inn, reading *1661* as *IGGI*. He still calls it that and always calls or texts his sister to say he is there, recalling fond childhood memories with her of days gone by.

Delightful mimosas, made-to-order omelets, fresh catch blue fish, and everything else we could want for breakfast left us sated, ready for the next item on the agenda for the day. It was off to the state beach, to find the best spot for doing nothing for the entire day but enjoying the best view, beach, ocean and companionship. The only real work was taking turns bartending rum and cokes and going to the snack bar for greasy burgers and fries.

Little did we know that we basked in paradise on that beach with a silent death threat.

That had to be when the tick bite occurred.

Two weeks later, Tom was very sick. He had flu-like symptoms and a fever that grew stronger every hour. At two a.m., when his fever hit one hundred and four degrees, I decided we needed to go to the emergency room.

It was quiet that night and he was seen quickly. After some fast blood work, an hour later the doctor informed us that Tom had Ehrlichiosis, an acute infection not unlike Lyme Disease, caused by the bite of a tiny, Lone Star tick.

We live in tick country; Lyme Disease was named for Lyme, Connecticut. We knew to check ourselves after we took a walk in the countryside or worked in the yard. We knew that a red ring on a bite area was a sure sign of a tick bite, and that you needed to see a doctor immediately for antibiotics.

But Tom did not have a red ring, nor did he feel or see a bite on his body.

What we didn't know, but later learned, is that Ehrlichiosis-transmitting ticks are also Lyme Disease transmitters. For this reason, patients with Ehrlichiosis should also be tested for Lyme, because the likelihood of coinfection is high. The Lone Star tick is the primary carrier. I thought they would be in Texas, but my research showed that the Lone Star tick is prominent in Block Island.

Who knew that ticks would be in the sand at the beach? I would never have thought to use tick or bug spray at the beach. Yet I felt responsible. That's where it had to have happened, since we didn't go hiking and, except for our time on the beach, we had been indoors.

The good news was that the doctor said this was not a form of Lyme Disease, it should clear up quickly with a course of antibiotics, and there would be no long-term effects. He was almost right. Three weeks of antibiotics and Tom was as good as new.

Since we had closed the restaurant, Tom was unemployed and antsy to do something. It started out like the classic Beatles song, "Nowhere Man." He was certainly going nowhere, with no plans, even though Tom could accomplish anything in the world he wanted.

Although he had been a chef for thirty years, it was time to move on to something different. Tom decided to start a new career, with much encouragement from me, learning the commercial voiceover business. He had a hearty, resounding, sexy voice that matched his personality. It jumped off the page to grab your full attention and make you smile. Everyone he met felt the same way. He was excited about a new career and an opportunity to make a difference in this field.

He took classes in New York City and practiced his new craft, sending out voiceover samples to potential employers. I tried to help with ideas of how he could promote himself and how he could sell his voiceovers. I was convinced that with his persona, he could fill the airwaves as soon as he received his first gig. But as time went by and there were no bites, his optimism ebbed. He stopped pursuing it on a daily, then a weekly basis.

I knew something was changing in him, but I had no idea what was really happening to his body, his person, his soul.

It was at this time, January of 2012, that Tom's voice started to change. There was a slight slur when he talked. At first, neither of us paid any attention, and then it was obvious it was not going away anytime soon. His friends thought he was drinking all day, since he did not have a job, and that caused the slurring. The first thing I always do is research, but nothing made any sense. It was time to go back to the doctor.

Tom went to his family practitioner, Dr. A, who ran blood tests and diagnosed him with Lyme Disease. Dr. A prescribed a six-week course of antibiotics. But this time, unlike the Erlichiosis meds, the antibiotics did not make a difference.

Dr. A did not schedule a follow-up visit, which should have been standard protocol, but Tom was nonplussed. He made an appointment, and the doctor prescribed another course of antibiotics, but only after our request. I wondered who the real doctor was.

I am still very bitter about how Dr. A handled Tom's illness. I asked him to find a better doctor who cared about his welfare, but I could only express my opinion which did not make a difference.

The slurring continued.

Dr. A eventually recommended Tom see a neurologist.

This was the beginning of many, many doctors, theories and treatments. We were sent into the vortex of the medical field to be whirled about in pandemonium. We became a number in a world that we wanted no part of and had no control over.

Tom made an appointment with a local neurologist that Dr. A recommended, but he did not want me to go with him. I know now that he had an inkling of what was to come, and he wanted to protect me from it firsthand. He was always thinking of me and trying to protect me as much as he could.

When I came home from work that day, Tom was sitting quietly, without any television or music on, which was not like him at all. He normally had SportsCenter on or forties music in the background, while he read the paper or did the *New York Times* crossword puzzle. Today was different.

I came in to a darkened room. He hugged and kissed me and told me he loved me.

Then he recounted the doctor's visit in a somber monotone—a slow, slurred voice. "The doctor discounted Lyme Disease and said he thought I might have ALS, Amyotrophic Lateral Sclerosis."

I had never heard of this, but Tom had. He knew. From his sports background, he knew it as Lou Gehrig's disease.

He sighed, put his arm around me and looked me straight in the eyes. He said, "There's no cure, and it's a death sentence."

The world stood still. I could not breathe. This could not be true. It had to be from the Lyme Disease. This could not be happening to us.

Chapter Seven
2012
A Bad Dream

Something is very different...

MY EYES FIXED ON HIS. I TRIED TO SEE A BETTER truth inside him. My voice would not work. I whispered the only question I could safely ask, "Do you think this could be true?"

"No, I don't, but something is very different in my body and I don't know, I just don't know."

Small things were happening to him that were indicators of something changing him inside out. When we slept at night, with my arms around him, I remembered feeling random vibrations of his body, like an intermittent battery that pulsed on and off when you least expected it. It didn't make any sense. Until now.

I didn't know what to think. My mind rushed with random crazy thoughts. *How could this be true? Why us? I can't accept this. It's a bad dream. I need to be strong for him.* My mind would not stop reeling in circles of denial, fear, and love for him.

We held each other with a grip that would last us a lifetime. We hugged and told each other that no matter what, we would fight it and be strong together and do what we needed to survive.

We sat there holding each other until dusk settled and the moon came out to shine on us, sharing words of love and hope and how our strength together would fight whatever would come our way. That night we went from the deepest darkness to a small bright star of hope and love.

There is nothing that can prepare you for the reality that the love of your life has a terminal disease. My immediate reaction was to find a solution. To find a way to stop it. To find a way to make it all better. When you are faced with the reality of death, you have two choices. Accept it, lie down and die or fight it with every weapon in your arsenal and hope that somehow, someway this will not be a death sentence.

Positive attitude is more than half the battle in any terminal disease. When I was diagnosed with breast cancer ten years ago, I made the immediate decision to fight this disease with every last ounce of strength I could muster to win the battle.

I researched diligently online and bought *Dr. Susan Love's Breast Book*. This book is about five inches thick. I read it front to back three times. I needed to know anything and everything about the disease they said I had. It made me feel as if I had control of my destiny. Reality dictates that you don't, but I could be knowledgeable, have a positive attitude and plan on not dying.

My takeaway on living a better life after I became a survivor is to take care of yourself, go to the doctor for checkups when you are supposed to, take vitamins, eat healthy, exercise, smile, and love. Use prevention from sun, bugs, disease and known harmful things. Most of all, keep a positive attitude. I did that with a non-acceptance of the fate that could have been mine. Most people will look at the dismal statistics of their diagnosis and prepare to die. They will make their wills, bucket lists, have a dour attitude and give up on life. I'm here to talk about it now, and I am a better person for taking an optimistic stance.

I have always said that cancer was the best thing that ever happened to me. It made me humble, appreciate everything I had, and allowed me not to worry about what I didn't have. I decided to just be happy with who I was and to live out however many days I had left on this earth with a smile on my face and in my heart. That served me well then, and up to now.

I wished it were me; I had the experience and the fight to deal with a terminal disease. Though I could not fathom how we would get through this, I knew our love would help us. I am an eternal optimist. Not only will I always see a glass half-full, I will expect it to magically become fuller the next time I look at it.

Chapter Eight
2012

Research

I have been known to make things happen that were impossible.

I WAS A FEROCIOUS FIEND RESEARCHER. I NEEDED to find a solution. I needed to save him. I devoured the Internet looking for everything I could find on ALS and Lyme Disease. The more I read, the more terrified I was. ALS is a terrible disease.

Amyotrophic comes from the Greek language: *A* means no or negative. *Myo* refers to muscle. *Trophic* means nourishment.

No muscle nourishment. When a muscle has no nourishment, it atrophies or wastes away. Lateral identifies the areas in a person's spinal cord where portions of the nerve cells that signal and control the muscles are located. As this area degenerates, it leads to scarring or hardening (sclerosis) in the region. It is estimated that 5,600 people are diagnosed every year, two out of 100,000 people.

The small amount of research done over the past fifty years has not found a cure. Since the ALS population is only about 30,000 at any time, it has not been a worthy investment for the pharmaceutical companies. Thirty thousand people are not enough to save; it is all about making money. Their lives do not count. Many studies and trials are done, but nothing substantial enough to make a difference.

There is a drug, Riluzole, that could help to extend life by two, maybe three months, but the side effects and the extension of life just adds one to two more months of agony.

In this day and age, how could this be true? It was unbelievable. More than half of all ALS patients might live three or more years after diagnosis. Twenty percent live five years or more; a small percentage might live more than ten years.

Once you are diagnosed, you become an outcast from the medical field. When you are diagnosed with this disease and its very short life span, there is no urgency or need to save your life. This was unbelievable! Unthinkable!

I learned that Stephen Hawking is the anomaly in the ALS statistics. He outlived all ALS patients on record and is a scientific curiosity. He proved that ALS is not one disease. He was diagnosed at the age of twenty-one and celebrated his seventy-fifth birthday in 2017. His mind was sharp as ever until his final day in March of 2018. How did Stephen Hawking live past seventy with ALS?

We learned that Riluzole (Rilutek1) was only one medication approved by the Food and Drug Administration for ALS. Rilutek, also known by its generic name of Riluzole, is the only medication that is FDA-approved specifically for the systemic treatment of ALS (as opposed to medications that are approved only to treat particular ALS symptoms, such as Nuedexta). Rilutek helps to slow down the progression of ALS/MND and prolong survival. However, it is not a cure for ALS, and it does not reverse the nerve damage or muscle weakness characterized by the disease. Rilutek may increase survival by three to five months.

According to the Mayo Clinic, Riluzole "appears to slow the disease's progression in some people, perhaps by reducing levels of glutamate," a chemical messenger in the brain. In people with ALS, it is often present in higher levels. The Mayo Clinic information said that the side effects of the drug were dizziness and gastrointestinal issues and possibly liver damage.

Everything I read confirmed that a person would degenerate slowly but surely. And there was nothing to be done except make the patient as comfortable as possible, until he could not breathe anymore.

I could not accept any of this.

My research uncovered a major controversy over the diagnosis of Lyme Disease versus ALS. There are theories that Lyme Disease will affect the central nervous system exactly how ALS does, and vice versa. On the Internet, I found an article written by a doctor named Martin Atkinson-Barr. He published a study that established a direct correlation between Lyme Disease and ALS.

Then I read a newspaper article from the Huffington Post: "Man Diagnosed with ALS Dies of Lyme Disease." It was about a Rhode Island man and backed up what Dr. Atkinson-Barr was saying. This article frames the idea that ALS and Lyme Disease both affect the central nervous system, which can lead to a misdiagnosis of either ALS or Lyme Disease because of the degenerative similarities.

The most frightening article I read was by Margaret Wahl in the *MDA/ALS Newsmagazine*: "ALS Doesn't Masquerade as Lyme Disease, Experts Say." This article illustrates the ongoing debate in the medical world that ALS and Lyme Disease are related. There are two opposite sides and opinions with the patient ping ponging between them.

You can stick your head in a dark hole and never deal with it, you can make believe that nothing is wrong, or you can face it straight on and feel like you can make a difference. I chose to learn everything I could, to decide how to fight, while being positive and optimistic we could beat this somehow, someway; even if the research did not tell me that story.

So, I chose to go with the direct correlation theory of Dr. Atkinson-Barr that this could be Lyme Disease, not ALS. There were no other options. If only this could be true. I needed to grab onto something that would give us hope. I prayed this would be the long straw that could save Tom's life.

I have been known to make impossible things happen, and I would give everything I had to do the same here. Fire brimmed in my eyes and my heart, facing this beast, trying to save my love. The most important thing was to protect him as much as I could from this horrid disease and to make him as comfortable and happy as he could be. Hopefully my optimism would rub off on him. I put on those rose-colored glasses with a passion in my soul.

Dr. B, his initial neurologist, called Tom with our first good news. "Tom, I am happy to report that your brain MRI shows normal results. This is encouraging news, but you should finish your course of antibiotics and then see how you feel."

This was our first glimmer of hope. We danced, celebrating, choosing to stay in this positive moment.

Dr. B did not schedule a follow-up appointment. How and why is that possible, I wondered? I decided it made sense to find a Lyme Literate doctor to explore how to conquer the Lyme Disease first. If that was eliminated, perhaps Tom would be on the road to good health again. My research did not produce an easy route. Looking for a doctor the medical profession did not endorse was precarious. It felt like looking for a quack to save a life. Crazy! It seemed like it was voodoo medicine.

I started with: How to Find a Lyme Literate Doctor (LLMD) in Your Area. This was the underground of the medical world. They kept a low profile and were extremely hard to find. Then I found: "About the Doctor Referral" (Lyme Disease Association). Finally, an organized listing, making it easier to find a Lyme Literate doctor, but there was still a stigma attached to these professionals, who were in high demand.

How will I ever find the right person? If only I could get a recommendation from someone.

As luck would have it, I ran into a friend who told me about Dr. C, who had helped him beat his severely debilitating Lyme Disease after only one year of treatment. He was miraculously back to normal. I was extremely hopeful that Tom could be, too. It was a significant sign to have a recommendation for a Lyme Literate doctor with positive results.

The first day we met with Dr. C, in August of 2012, Tom was in good spirits, joking and being positive that the doctor could help him get rid of this once and for all. His slurring had worsened, and one side of his face had fallen a bit, but otherwise he was in good form and still living life large.

I always wanted Tom to be in charge, to kick things off with the doctors we saw. It gave them a good understanding about his current state and his precious personality.

"Hello, Doc, how are you today?"

Dr. C replied, "I'm fine, but I need to know how you feel today."

"Today is a good day, but this slur is getting in the way of my comedy act. Do you think you could do something about that?" Tom was on stage, playing the role of his life, working toward the finale where we both live happily ever after.

Dr. C narrowed his eyes, as if hoping for something serious, and asked me, "Can you give me his history?"

I replied parrot-like, repeating the dissertation of Tom's medical history, along with a printed timeline of dates, diagnosis, test results, and opinions.

The doctor examined Tom, asking several questions, taking extensive blood to test for several forms of Lyme Disease. He felt he could help us. A glimmer of hope grew a tiny bit brighter.

Our forty-five-minute drive for the return visit and results was somber; we both contemplated, in our own minds, what the results might be. Tom was probably thinking the worst, and I was thinking the best possible result.

Whenever we went to a new doctor, we had unspoken reverence for the possibility of a cure. We would look at each other with soulful, hopeful eyes, holding hands, pressing it just so—to let each other know that we hoped and prayed this would be the one. The words need not be spoken.

Dr. C was upbeat. He diagnosed Tom with Clinical Lyme, Babesiosis, Bartonella and Ehrlichiosis. He concluded that these various types of Lyme Disease had the effect that Tom was experiencing. He started another course of antibiotics, along with some natural compounds to help his system. Tom gladly started the antibiotics again. We also started probiotics to counter the side effects of the antibiotics.

Confident we had found someone who could help us, we felt giddy with relief.

Chapter Nine
2012

The Fight

The medical ward was open for business.

FIGHTING FOR ANYTHING WORTHWHILE REQUIRES guts, patience and an infinite amount of confidence that you will win the battle. I was not a patient person, but I was being forced to learn how to be one.

After the first course of antibiotics, Tom's energy level and how he felt improved, but the slurring became drunker and drunker. I wondered if I would understand him better if I was drunk.

The new course of antibiotics did not work. His fingers started to cripple, forming perfect Cs. Creative handling of a pen or a chef's knife allowed him to carry on with crossword puzzles and cooking, two things he truly enjoyed and was especially good at. Nothing stopped him from doing what he loved.

In October, Dr. C recommended a stronger antibiotic course of intravenous antibiotic with Ceftriaxone, due to the amount of different difficult strains of the disease in his system. Alarms should have gone off. We should have been asking why he was not getting better, but we followed the doctor's recommendation, thinking it normal and required. Why would we question his expert opinion?

Tom had a PICC line inserted to allow him to self-medicate every day. This required a weekly nurse visit to verify that there was no infection, flush the line, and report back to the doctor on the status of the patient. The first box of medical supplies and equipment arrived and found an inconspicuous home in the corner of the dining room.

The medical ward was open for business.

Life fell into a comfortable rhythm for several months of antibiotic treatment. It could be the magic potion to cure Tom, just like it had for several other people we knew who had bad cases of Lyme Disease. In hindsight, we should have been alarmed that this was necessary, but a feeling of comfort and contentment came with each treatment. This could be the answer to everything; we were diligent and hopeful. Tom's role changed from job-hunting to nursing 101.

Tom stayed at home, starting his day by reading the *New York Times* cover to cover. He was an avid reader of the obituaries and often saved the ones he thought I would enjoy reading. It is amazing the things you learn about people from their obituaries. He always saved the artist obits and famous business people that my company might have been associated with. He still thoroughly enjoyed the challenge of the *NYT* crosswords, like a brain surgeon. Folding the paper exactly the same way every day, with very crisp corners and folds, starting at the top left corner and working his way from left to right across the entire block, Tom balanced the pencil between his pointer and middle finger to scratch out the fate of empty squares.

I liked to think of him as a brain surgeon because his brain was razor sharp and precise with quick knowledge.

Sometimes we would have timed races to finish a puzzle. There was no competition. Tom was always the winner. Even though his body was eroding, his mind was keen as ever.

I often wondered how he felt at these times: ill and not able to live a normal life? Or was he happy for the relief of not having to deal with life, content to be in this nice cozy place called Home Sweet Home?

Fortunately, my job was only five minutes away. The days turned into a yo-yo routine of back and forth between home and work.

Work started for me at eight a.m., while Tom was still asleep. Noontime would bring me home to a lovely lunch prepared by Chef Tom. It could be chicken salad with tarragon, grapes, and dried cranberries, or a decadent corned beef Reuben just like he used to serve at our restaurant, which was billed as "The Best Reuben You Ever Had." And it was.

I always asked the question, "Honey, where are we going today?"

Recorded *House Hunters International* episodes gave us our daily escape to a different country to see what life could be like there. It was our way of traveling together from our living room. The magic of travel came alive every day. If our heritage countries of Italy or Ireland came on, we were enamored all the more. We would vote on which house the couple would pick and then debate on where we would have lived if we were there.

Life was good as it could be.

Back to work I would go and come home in time for dinner and our sacred *Jeopardy!* routine. Tradition demanded cheese and crackers with a Proper Cocktail (PC) prepared just prior to starting time. This stemmed from the days

Glaze: (can be made a day in advance)
3 jiggers bourbon
1 cup molasses
½ cup orange juice
2 cups water
½ tsp. allspice
1 tsp. ginger
1 cup brown sugar
Place all ingredients into a thick stovetop pot. Bring to boil and lower to a simmer allowing to reduce by ½.
Put in fridge and reheat next day

Sweet potatoes:
5 sweet potatoes
5 tbl. Butter
½ tsp. white pepper
Salt to taste
¼ tsp. Nutmeg
Hot chicken stock
Peel potatoes and cook until fork tender and drain. Put back in same pot and mash with next four ingredients. When thoroughly mashed check for consistency and add (a little at a time because you can always add but you can never take away) until you are happy with the texture.

Cranberry vinaigrette: (can be made a day or two ahead)
2 tbl. Cranberry frozen concentrate (use the rest for Cape Cod Mimosas in the morning)
½ cup white wine vinegar
Oregano ¼ tsp. dry 1tsp. Fresh
1 ½ cup olive oil
Salt and pepper
Combine first 3 ingredients the slowly add olive oil while whisking until fully emulsed. Add salt and pepper to taste

Salad:
1 head romaine
1 head red leaf
Small red onion
½ English cucumber
Rinse all produce and cut to desired size. Just before service toss all ingredients including dressing and candied walnuts and plate. (you can use the wet leftover salad in an omelet the next morning along with anything else in your fridge. Enjoy with your Mimosas!!!)

Tom Kilmurray is the owner and executive chef of The Opera Café in Bethel, Ct

"Tom, can you please, please, please reconsider documenting your incredible recipes for a cookbook?"

No response.

"This would give you something to do and when we published it, the world would be a better place. I will help you, if you will let me?"

Tom made that face he always made when he didn't want to do something. His eyes would narrow, and his cheeks suck in like he was holding his breath, hoping the question would evaporate into thin air. I could see his brain spinning to figure out how to get me off this subject again.

Finally, he said, "I don't want to." It was the same answer, again and again.

"But, why? You have never given me a reason why. Why don't you want to document your recipes and preserve them for everyone who loves them and loves you?"

Tom knew I would never stop asking.

"Because I am a failed chef. I could not even keep a restaurant running, why would anyone in their right mind want my recipes? I'm not good enough."

It felt like being punched in the stomach, feeling his shame and pain. "I strongly disagree. Losing the restaurant had nothing to do with your exceptional talent as a chef; it was the economy that undid us. Just promise me you will think about it, for me."

There was a time I was not allowed in the kitchen when he was cooking, since he needed all the space and did not want me to interfere. My cooking skills were considered inferior for this chef. Necessity changed his mind.

I was casually asked to help in a professional way. "Jo Ann, how would you like to be my Sous Chef and Jardinière tonight?"

"Wow, I would love to help out in your kitchen, Chef."

The evolution of change started with passing the gauntlet in his kitchen to prep vegetables, fish and meat, and to create the salads. It was too tedious for him to use the chef's knife. This was wonderful for me because he taught me so much about cooking and the nuances that only a chef can know. His watchful eyes were always on my work to insure the quality of the results. I know it was extremely hard for him to give up the control of the kitchen, his domain, and to allow me to help him; but these became precious times for us that I will always savor.

We fell into a rhythm of medications, treatments and daily life, almost like living in a cozy cocoon of positive feelings, while closing our eyes to everything and everyone except our little world.

We didn't talk about it, but these were the weeks and the months that hope cheered us on: this treatment for a cure of the Lyme Disease to prove it was not ALS.

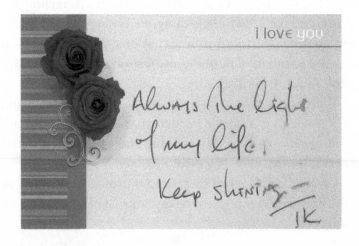

We had always been social animals and, during this time, Tom seemed to want to socialize more than usual. We would go to parties, host dinner parties, go to music events, and spend time with family both near and far. I was happy to see him involved with the world and feeling optimistic. Whenever we went somewhere, people would ask how he was doing. We would both revert to the drill that he was doing okay, continuing with IV antibiotics and we hoped for the best.

The IV antibiotic treatment continued through the holidays and into the New Year of 2013, but Tom had stopped improving.

Tom suggested a road trip in December to see his grandmother Mimi in Cleveland; and to meet in the middle with my daughter, son-in-law and two grandchildren who lived in Michigan. I always wondered if he ultimately knew how this story would end, and he needed to see and touch certain people before he died.

We had devised the meet in the middle plan to shorten each other's driving time to only six hours instead of twelve, and to stay somewhere with amenities. This trip was to a Pennsylvania resort, to celebrate birthdays, Thanksgiving and Christmas all in one with my daughter's family, and the next stop in Cleveland.

Traditionally, we visited Mimi for the Fourth of July holiday, but we couldn't due to Tom's treatment, so we took advantage of being so close and planned on going to celebrate her hundred-and-first birthday. The trip would be good for Tom's spirit, his conscience and soul, as well as mine.

We arrived at our "meet in the middle" resort in Pennsylvania. There is nothing like children to make you feel better about anything. Hugs and kisses with everyone, unloading the presents, turkey, groceries with everything for a traditional Thanksgiving dinner. I situated Tom on the couch to get settled and ready for his treatment.

My daughter Jen and her husband Greg took me aside outside and expressed their shock at how Tom looked. They knew he was sick with Lyme Disease, but they were not prepared for how much weight he had lost and how he had changed.

He was still Tom Tom to the kids, but he had shrunk to almost half of the burly, rough-and-tumble memory they had of him. This change was not only in his body, but his spirit as well. I can remember many nights with the kids crawling all over him on the couch, just cavorting as big and little kids do. They still stuck to him like glue, but it was with caresses, hand-holding and a bond that was soft and smooth as a purring kitten in your lap.

Since I saw him every day, I didn't really notice the gradual changes. It was a big wake-up call for me to see their shock and to put things in perspective. I decided then and there that when we got home, we needed to look for another course of action. I was concerned that I was falling into those rose-colored glass sentiments way too much.

We had a very merry three days. Day one was all about celebrating everyone's birthday with candles, cakes, presents and a special dinner. We dressed up in our holiday finery to make it even more festive. Luciano's was a fabulous Italian restaurant in town that everyone recommended. It was funny that the one word Tom could say enormously well was Luciano's. He rolled it off his tongue loud and long with an Italian accent, even though he was Irish to the bone.

The owner joined us at our table to wish us well and gave us each a jar of their famous Luciano tomato sauce. It was a special evening with everyone in the restaurant commenting to us on how beautiful the children were and what a lovely family we had. I could not have agreed more.

Day two was Thanksgiving, resplendent with turkey and all the fixings. Tom was in charge of the turkey timing and offered his advice on every other dish that Jen and I made:

"Make sure you don't overboil the potatoes, they should be fork tender."

"Who's making the gravy? I need to supervise."

It was exactly the way Thanksgiving should be. When we finally sat down to a bountiful table with our family around it, holding hands, giving thanks for this food, family and time together, we also prayed for Tom's health more than anything else.

Naps were in store for most, except for Esther and Elijah, who decorated their own Christmas trees, since we decided it was now Christmas Eve. As tradition had it, one or two presents are opened on Christmas Eve, which was always holiday jammies for the kids and something else special. This year, fuzzy animals with glow light to be night lights were a hit. Then off to bed to wait for Christmas morning.

Tom and I stayed up and had his famous TK coffee, named after him, consisting of coffee, Irish whiskey, Irish cream, whipped cream, fresh nutmeg and a cherry on top . . . delicious. We shared the special moments we were enjoying together with our family, feeling content.

Day three was our early Christmas Day. Happy children bounded down the stairs bright and early to find lots of presents. Then we were all off to the resort lodge for breakfast with Santa. Tom was a sport to participate for a short while to enjoy the thrill of the children.

The lodge had a spectacular view of the lake, setting a perfect backdrop for Santa and his merry Elves and making it feel as if we were at the North Pole. These were memorable times, especially for Tom, that we would always have in our hearts. The excitement of the three days meant naps for everyone, treatment for Tom, and me packing up for the next leg of our trip, to visit Mimi in Cleveland. Tom was tired, but really looking forward to this visit, since he was Mimi's first grandchild and they adored each other. But I could see his energy draining faster than usual.

I love Mimi. She has all her wits about her. She can remember everything in her life and loves to regale you with fascinating stories. She lives in a high-rise penthouse apartment that overlooks Lake Erie and the Cleveland skyline. She is the matriarch of the building. Everyone there knows her and loves her. What is not to love? She is charming, dignified, beautiful, funny, and has a mind of her own. She grew up in a different era and has evolved into this time but has never left the past behind.

The elevator took us to the twelfth floor, and we walked down the long hallway to the door Mimi kept unlocked when we were in town. As we walked through the door we transitioned to a different time. Twenty-five years fell away. Everything was exactly as it was on our last visit and on every visit. I couldn't imagine it any other way. The decor was tasteful with fine furniture, paintings, and delightful collections of photographs, jade, silver and equestrian details. There was no sound except the tick-tock of the grandfather clock that stood guard in the dining room. It was as if no one was home.

"Hello, Mimi, we are here!" I introduced our arrival.

"Well, thank God you are finally here. I am in the den,"

she shouted. There was always some shouting at Mimi's since her apartment was so large.

We made our way to the den to find her in her favorite chair, sitting in silence, waiting for us. This room was the most used room, decorated with anything and everything equestrian. The walls were painted a kelly green that reminded me of being on golf course greens and at the club. Pictures of Mimi's beloved horse, Tom, and her as a teenager, hang prominently on the wall, along with framed prints of gallant horses. Of course, there were many pictures on tables of family, surrounding her, keeping her company. It was a comforting place to be.

We all hugged, kissed and didn't want to let go. It warmed my heart to see them together, Mimi and Tom. I have seen them relate to each other on so many levels, like the drinks they enjoy and the foods that they love: lamb chops, crab cakes, and simple kielbasa with mashed potatoes. They were both born aristocrats, and their charming air of distinction warmed their personalities.

This visit they had something else to relate to, which was their mortality. They didn't talk about it in those words, but as they looked at each other and held each other's hands, it seemed as if it might be the last time.

These types of moments make you realize your entire life is made up of precious moments. Everyone has a collection of the best moments in their lives that sit next to the worst moments.

Which ones to keep? I tend to file the bad boys in the dark recesses of my brain and hope I never have to go there again. I like being an eternal optimist. I needed to put on those rose-colored glasses and look for something, anything, to give us hope.

In my heart and soul, I felt like I might be biding time, but I knew that if I became negative, desolate and gave up that we would both die and never recover. I resolved to do anything and everything possible to save us both. If I couldn't save Tom physically, I could certainly save him mentally and lovingly.

Life at Mimi's was very typical, even at her age of one-hundred-and-one. She would rise fairly early, around eight, and expect everyone else to be up and ready for breakfast. She still had a good appetite and, when Tom was in the house, she expected and hoped he would cook a fabulous breakfast, as only he could. I decided to be the chef of the morning on this trip, to give Tom and Mimi some special time together. They loved it, and I enjoyed trying to meet Tom and Mimi's expectations for breakfast.

They were not disappointed, thank goodness, as we sat in the dining room with proper service and china, discussing the woes of the world. We enjoyed a delightful view of the Cleveland skyline bidding us good morning, with a graphic painting of buildings of every size and shape standing strong together.

After breakfast, it was naptime for Mimi and time for us to read or take a stroll around the property to enjoy the gorgeous views of Lake Erie and chat with the folks we knew there. Mimi lived in a wonderful place with all the accoutrements one could want. It was truly an enjoyable, relaxing time.

Dinner was an event. Cocktails were mandatory at five o'clock. Of course, everyone dressed for dinner. Since we were celebrating Mimi's birthday, we had a special delivery shipped in of her favorite caviar, which she adored. It was important to make Melba bread toast points for the caviar, which I did.

Mimi insisted on taking us downstairs to the restaurant for dinner. From the restaurant windows, we could see walking trails that circled the complex and skirted Lake Erie with its stunning panorama of sailboats and frothy waves. Just like an ocean, there was no end in sight. It was peaceful and captivating at the same time. On this cold day in December, I could imagine myself in one of those sailboats going to the edge of the end with my love. No one knew what was in store for us in those waves ahead.

Tom wore a jacket, as was only proper; even though it was big on him, he looked very handsome. I wore a dress that Mimi approved of (yeah!), and Mimi was dressed in her best jewels and finery. We were all excited about our special evening together.

Tom and Mimi traditionally both drank vodka in the summer and scotch in the winter, so scotch was supposed to be the drink of the day for them, but they both opted for a light vodka drink to pair well with the caviar. I drink vodka year-round.

Vodka and caviar were served by one of the wonderful women who served as twenty-four-hour help for her. Mimi was delighted. She was a little girl with the best present anyone could have ever given her. It was so wonderful to see her absolute delight and Tom's wonderment of her. It was a memory I will never forget.

She entertained us with stories about when she had caviar in many different countries and places, and how she loved it so much. We were captured in her past, feeling part of her life and her loves.

We asked her to recite the poem she wrote about her horse, Tom. She did perfectly:

Silver Tom

There is nothing I like better than riding in the rain,
With Silver Tom beneath me we sail down our lover's lane,
The drops all gleam like diamonds in his lovely silver mane,
There is a certain brook we know where big frogs croak all day,
But we're such frequent callers that when we come, they stay,
Ah, we come home like two great kings,
Rain always makes my Tommy act as though we were on wings,
For now, I have diamonds in my hair like those sprinkled in his mane,
There's nothing I like better than riding in the rain.

Applause and accolades for Mimi's performance filled our hearts with joy.

Dinner was wonderful with great conversation, more perfect pictures of Tom and Mimi together, then up to bed after a long, wonderful day.

We stayed another day and a half before our drive back and had more of the same, with dinner at home instead of downstairs, but always wonderful.

Our final dinner played like a goodbye scene in a properly staged setting with good food, music in the background, friends wishing you well in a lovely restaurant. When I saw Tom and Mimi staring into each other's eyes like they would never see each other again, I wanted to stop time forever, freeze-frame the movie. But, I had no control over that camera.

The rest of our time with Mimi was delightfully heartwarming and dear to both Tom and me. Unfortunately, it was time to return to our reality and face the music, whatever would be playing when we got there. It was a bittersweet departure with long hugs and many tears from all of us.

The ten-hour ride home was somewhat quiet, with Tom and I with our own thoughts. I thought hard about Tom's current medical status and how he was not getting better. I needed to find answers to this mystery. I knew that I was the only one who could find a way, find a solution, and I was determined to do that when we got home. I could not let things get worse.

Chapter Ten
Coulda, Shoulda, Woulda

Although he did rub off on me . . .

PATIENCE IS A GIFT.

It was a learned gift that was delivered when I had no choice.

Could I have done something different, sooner, better?

Could there be a magic potion somewhere that could be a cure?

Should I be more or less patient with the medical world?

Should we just give up?

Would it have helped us both if we just accepted the hand that was dealt to us?

Would less patience with the situation solve this medical mystery sooner?

The questions were endless. During that long ride from Cleveland, my mind roamed the highways and byways of what to do. We had been down several roads without satisfactory results. I knew there were many roads yet to follow, some more distressing than others, but which ones were the right ones for us, now?

I wished I could be as casual and nonchalant about this illness as Tom seemed to be. His manner read like nothing was wrong and life was good. I wished I felt the same.

A stranger meeting him for the first time would appreciate his good nature and natural glow of a happy life. They would be shocked to learn how sick he really was.

He did rub off on me in some ways, though. I'm not sure if my patience was earned, learned or borrowed from Tom, but it allowed me to slow down my thoughts to better ways of thinking. I learned to be open to other ideas, things, and people. Close-mindedness is a nasty disease. Tom was the most open-minded person I know. He forced me to question the fabric of my thinking. He seemed to have that soft, luxurious outlook of a lacy silk, despite being a big hunk o' man you would never imagine wearing anything lacy or silky. But the way he approached ideas or people had always been without effort or concern.

I, on the other hand, had always been starched cotton. There is nothing wrong with starched cotton, but the stiffness I carried caused hesitation and procrastination that would not allow me to follow my dreams. I learned by being with Tom that going with the flow is much more satisfying and fun than slamming the door on an adventure with a closed mind and heart.

Just going on this trip to visit the kids and Mimi at a moment's notice illustrated our adventurous spirit together, without a care for any illness that might hold us back. Tom's illness took a back seat to living life. Nothing could be wrong if you believed that today we could enjoy our family and spend happy moments together that will forever be locked in the treasure chest of love. My starch had gone, and the cotton turned into something much more exotic and soft.

Of course, he was off the charts open in a way I could never be, with my Catholic upbringing and feeling the burden of responsibilities. But he allowed me to see how easier life could be, if you just opened your mind and allowed life to walk you down that happy trail. Learning how to be patient and open-minded made me a better person and mate to carry Tom through.

Although, as contradictory as it seems, when I was in high school I was considered one of the wild and crazy kids. We were kind of hippies in our own way. We were suburban hippies who went to good schools and came from "proper-manners-please" families.

My last thought on that very quiet drive home was that patience could become an excellent procrastination tool.

I would put patience in my pocket until I needed to use it. But charging ahead without delay was needed now.

Chapter Eleven
2012

More Research

We needed to do this ASAP.

OUR RETURN BROUGHT US BACK TO OUR DAILY routine, although nothing was routine about Tom's health. The voice of logic in my head shouted: *Do something! Do something, anything, just do it!*

Tom's health was failing faster than before. It was like that snowball rolling down the mountain, gaining speed and growing larger every day. His hands became crippled and more useless. For the first time in his life, food did not interest him. Sleeping and resting became the main events of the day.

The Lyme Disease treatment for the past year gave Tom some high roads of improvements and some fast curves, but it seemed that now it was all downhill.

It was time to call in the cavalry, or whomever I could find to fight the battle. I felt overwhelmed and frightened. I did not know what to do. I had no one to turn to.

I felt the weight of the world on my shoulders. I was the only one who could possibly help him, and I didn't have the resources available to point me in the right direction. I could only rely on my instincts, my research, my common sense and my gut feel for what was the right or wrong thing to do. I thought about it constantly, day and night. It was always on my mind. What can I do? How can I solve this mystery? How could I save the love of my life?

The middle of the night found me on the Internet doing more research, because I could not sleep.

Research on the Internet is like putting together a 10,000-piece puzzle. You have to do so many different searches to get to the information you need. It takes hours and hours of research to put together the pieces of something that comes close to any sense. This research required patience I did not normally have.

When the picture started coming together, I just wanted to run away from it as fast as I could. You can't believe everything you read on the Internet, but the reality is you must, because you don't have anything else. The doctors we had dealt with so far could not solve this situation. It was not that they didn't care; they just did not know how to save Tom.

So, I resolved to continue my research, form opinions and make lists of options, while Tom faded away day by day.

Of course, Tom had final say in all of it. But he was not in the thick of things trying to find a solution. If anything, he was indifferent to it. I would give him articles to read or websites to review and he would take a quick look to appease me, but he was not interested.

I couldn't figure out if he could not deal with reading this terrible stuff, or if he felt confident in my handling it and just giving him recommendations. I always presented the pros and cons and tried to discuss what options we had.

So, in the end, he did receive all the information, through me. This was my challenge: to keep us afloat on this sea of uncertainty. There was always the possibility that he accepted his fate but participated because he didn't want me to give up my crusade to save him. He knew that if I didn't have hope, I would die, too.

I held my anguish inside of me, tightly rolled, holding my breath. Every new search gave me something that might be a solution. When it wasn't, I kept going, again and again. I needed to find something, anything that could be the game changer. If I couldn't do this, I would not be able to live with myself, look myself in a mirror or ever feel capable again.

It would have been easier if we dealt with a black-and-white case, but we were not. This was as gray as gray could be—murky and covert—Lyme Disease versus ALS.

If it was ALS, it would be black as black can be. If it was Lyme Disease, it would be gray. These are two distinct diseases that have two distinct types of doctors and treatments or, in the case of ALS, non-treatment. Logic dictated that I should go down both paths separately, but I was desperate to find a cross section of both that could give me a miracle.

For instance, it made sense for Lyme Disease to get Tom speech, physical, and occupational therapy. But if he truly had ALS, this would be the worst thing for him, since it would use up his muscles sooner than later. An ALS patient does not do therapy at all. It promotes deterioration of the muscle instead of building them up.

A potentially damaging decision had to be made. My logic, and Tom agreed, was that if you don't use it, you lose it. It was a risk, but we needed to take risks and do what felt right at the time. Doing something rather than nothing felt better.

This was also a challenge in the world of insurance. Unless a doctor prescribes it, the insurance company will not pay for it. The only doctor we were dealing with at the time was our Lyme Literate doctor. He said yes, therapy was a great idea.

Therapy started with Tom driving the ten minutes to the location and spending an hour or two doing different therapies. I went on the first visits to translate for Tom. At this point, his speech was so bad that anyone who did not know him could not understand him. We joked that Tom had a whole new language called "Tomese." Once you learned it, it was easier to communicate.

The therapy appeared to be a great decision. He was getting out of the house three to four times a week, doing something to hopefully help him. Interaction with different people opened his world back up to help Tom feel human again. He had exercises to do at home in between sessions, and he felt it was helping. I did not see any difference, but he was happy and that's all that counted at the time.

When Tom decided he should not drive anymore, I would drop him off and pick him up. I was shocked that in the blink of an eye, Tom gave up driving. He loved to drive. I had been concerned he would have a hard time giving it up and would be upset, but he just stopped driving one day and never talked about it. He was very pragmatic about it—a Mimi trait. Amazing!

Sometimes I would stay to see the interaction and to see what was really happening at therapy. One time, his speech therapist took me aside and recommended Tom see a specific neurologist she knew and highly recommended. She felt he needed that kind of help.

Since I was already investigating neurologists, for me this was a sign from heaven that her doctor was the one we should see. He was local, perfect for another opinion. I called and made an appointment for the following week.

I learned more than I ever wanted to know about ALS, Lyme Disease and central nervous system diseases. What was the connection? Tom knew a small bit of information about ALS, and that was enough for him. He did not need any more fire on his wounds. I needed my fire to keep burning to try to figure out how to keep from losing him, while maintaining a positive attitude and eliminating negativity.

I continued my research of Lyme/ALS, which turned up an interesting find. Columbia University Medical Center in New York City had a Lyme and Tick-Borne Diseases Research Center. They were the only place that used ALS and Lyme Disease in the same sentence. They offered an evaluation for a fee to analyze the patient for physical and physiological status of Lyme or ALS and the impact to the patient. After all my months of research, the fact that I just found this now was unbelievable.

The website cautioned that there was a very long list of people waiting for an appointment and that you needed to be patient (no pun intended). I thought, where there is a will, there is a way. We needed to do this ASAP. The website said to call and leave a message and someday, potentially weeks later, someone would get in touch with you. This was not how I liked to get things done, but I had no choice in the matter. It was my new reality of not being in control.

I debated, should I, or should I not . . . should I, or should I not. I debated for a week and then finally decided I had no choice; why had I waited a whole week, just delaying the process? Did I fear the results and not want to hear the truth?

I decided I needed to do this for Tom and I needed to be brave and I also needed to be patient. I have never been a patient person, but now I had to figure out how to be patient. Before the illness, Tom would laugh at my impatience. It could be waiting in line at the grocery store or crossing a street with oncoming traffic.

"Jo Ann, what is your hurry? Why are you I such a rush? You have the rest of your life to do whatever you need to do. You get yourself so worked up, you are not enjoying the ride." This was Tom always in slow motion, unless he was cooking.

"Easy for you to say, since you are not the one doing what needs to get accomplished." I knew that was unfair, but true. I did not have time to wait.

So, I summoned my courage, my best voice-mail voice, my calm manner, and I made the call.

To my astonishment, a real person answered the phone. She was Dr. D, covering for the receptionist who was out sick. She told me she did not normally answer the phone.

I explained why I was calling and gave her detailed the information about my husband. She was extremely interested in his case and asked several questions. We talked about his situation for about twenty minutes; then to my surprise, she asked if we could come in for the evaluation in two weeks.

"Yes, of course!" I said, then I asked her, "Doctor, I thought that there was a long waiting list."

She chuckled. "Since I am the doctor, I decided to start at the bottom of the list today because Tom's is a special case that needs attention immediately."

I could barely speak. "Thank you very much, Doctor. I look forward to meeting you in two weeks. Thank you again."

This was our lucky day. Our worlds suddenly became an orbital collision course. Within three weeks, we would receive new results from our Lyme Literate Doctor, meet a new neurologist, and be evaluated by the Columbia University Medical Center. It was terrifying but satisfying. If we could find the truth, hopefully, we could save Tom.

The arrangements were made through the Christmas/New Year's holidays. It was extremely hard to be festive and happy when our entire world together was crumbling.

During that holiday season we enjoyed the grandchildren, our family and friends who helped us feel normal, but most of all we enjoyed each other. Those were the only gifts we needed.

It is amazing how your attitude will rub off on everyone. If you are okay, then everyone else will be okay, too. If you can't deal with what you are going through and don't want to partake in festivities or conversation, then everyone else drops into your state.

If your insides are aching with hurt and fear, the last thing you want to do is to paint your exterior with good tidings, positive energy and joy. We resolved to be healthy and happy in 2013 and appreciate everything good we had.

But in my heart and soul, I was afraid that we were in trouble.

The Doctor Maze

We were in shock . . .

THE IV ANTIBIOTIC TREATMENT CONTINUED
through the holidays and into the New Year of 2013, but
Tom had stopped improving. If anything, his symptoms
worsened. His swallowing became a problem and his
breathing was distressed if he exerted himself. The shadow
of ALS loomed larger.

The dawn of 2013 brought a whole new year to look forward to and to wonder how it would end. I have always
loved New Year's Day. You never have anywhere to be, and
you get to look down that large calendar and dream about
the possibilities. Is this the year to lose weight finally? To
go to Italy? What did we not do last year that we can do
this year? But this new year was different. All I could think
about was how could I save Tom.

I was not sure where we stood with ALS at this point.
The conclusion after discussion with Dr. C, the Lyme Literate doctor, was to wait for the results from the neurologist
and the Lyme Research Center.

Our first appointment of the new year was with the
local neurologist, Dr. E. With extreme trepidation, we

visited him the following week. We were greeted by a very gentle soul who had a small ponytail and a kind personality. He was not in a rush and showed interest in our story. I did most of the talking since Tom's speech had eroded to where most people could not understand him.

After hearing all the details, Dr. E examined Tom. When asked to lie down on the table, Tom could not breathe properly lying flat, so he was propped up. This was the first time I had seen this occur. It seems that he had managed this situation at home by ensuring he was always tilted to ease his breathing, without me knowing it.

Tom was down to his skivvies, and Dr. E asked him how long he had the fasciculations on his legs and arms . . . another detail I was not aware of. I was shocked.

Did I have blinders on or did Tom simply not want me to know these things? I was frightened to hear what the doctor would say.

He said the words no one ever wants to hear: "I strongly believe you have Amyotrophic Lateral Sclerosis or ALS. You have presented in a bulbar fashion, and it is seriously affecting your breathing functions."

I protested that Tom still tested positive for Lyme Disease.

Dr. E strongly discounted that, saying it had nothing to do with what is happening now. "The fasciculations, your breathing and speech impairments are all strong traits of ALS."

My worst fears were becoming a reality.

"This is my professional opinion, but I will recommend a second opinion and proper testing to confirm my judgment."

He gave us the name of Dr. F at the Hospital for Special Care in New Britain, Connecticut. He would call Dr. F and ask him to schedule an appointment for us as quickly as possible. He also insisted that we see a pulmonary specialist for Tom's breathing situation. He recommended Dr. G, and actually called him while we were there, to have an appointment made right away.

We were in shock, and drove home in silence. We sat on the couch and just held each other. And I cried.

Tom tried to calm me and tell me he loved me and was thankful that he had found me and our love, which made him complete and that he would love me forever, no matter what. I told him I would always be by his side, would love him forever and would try my best to change this, to find a way to make it different. If I could not do that, I would make it the best it could be for him.

We stayed there holding each other until the day ended and the moonlight was the only light to whisper to us. It did not cast any hope on us.

Since the first tick bite on Block Island and the first illness of Erlichiosis, Tom's spirit rarely fell; there were only a handful of low days. This was the lowest.

That night, after hours of contemplation, he told me that he had made a decision. If this was true, he did not want to die a horrible death. He decided that he would take his own life before a tragic end, and that he would recruit his brother Chris to help him if necessary. Chris, a veteran, had experienced death in his years of service in Iraq. He wanted me to know his wishes and to accept them as his wife.

I accepted what he wanted to do, with a protest that I could and should help him if necessary, not his brother. I was his wife. He appreciated me wanting to do that, but he did not want the guilt or horror of that left to me. He was afraid of how that would affect me and did not want to do that to me. I argued that I was in this for better or worse, 'til death do us part, and I could and would do this for him. I would do anything for him.

We agreed to disagree and to see what would happen— so long as I knew his wishes and he knew my feelings. We both felt better after this discussion, which was so typical of us. We would always debate in good form and then create a compromise, agreement or a plan.

This was nothing like that. This was a life and death decision.

The next day I woke with a need to make things better somehow. I was trying to imagine how I could possibly do that under these circumstances. I woke up early, made coffee, turned on forties music, fetched the paper, as we always did on Sunday. I tried to read the paper, but I couldn't concentrate. I could only think about Tom. What was I going to do? How was I going to act? How were we going to deal with this tragic news?

I knew I could not accept this diagnosis, this reality, but I would do anything and everything I could to make him comfortable, happy and loved.

Strength is an interesting thing. You don't know if you have it. You don't know how you get it. You can be afraid of spiders, like I am, but when tragedy strikes, somehow people find strength inside their bones. You have to dig deep in the recesses of your person to do that. I was digging for strength that day and I think I found it.

When Tom got up, we talked about hope, love and our future together, however short or long it might be. We put together his bucket list.

Tom's Bucket List 2-5-13

- ☐ Niagara Falls
- ☐ Cruise
- ☐ Cheese crepe in Paris
- ☐ Top of Empire State Building
- ☐ New York Yankees Stadium
- ☐ Hawaii

I was surprised at how short the list was. "Tom, why is your list so short?"

"Jo Ann, I have everything I always wanted right here, being with you, the love of my life, plus I've done mostly everything I ever wanted to do."

I couldn't argue with that. But still, I would make the rest of his life the best it could possibly be.

Chapter Thirteen
2013
Zigzag

They signed us up for another set of appointments . . .

OUR CALENDAR BECAME THE ZIG AND ZAG OF the doctor maze to find answers. The next appointment, in January, brought us to the pulmonary specialist, Dr. G. Our neurologist had discussed Tom's case with him ahead of time.

"Hello, I'm Dr. G. I'm so sorry that you have ALS." He was matter of fact without any consideration of circumstances and feelings. His only job was to solve Tom's breathing problems.

I could not believe this. Here we go again with everyone assuming something that is not proven. I objected. "Doctor, Tom has not been officially diagnosed with ALS, and he is still being treated for Lyme Disease and the various other strains, which is giving us conflicting opinions of what is wrong."

The doctor realized he had not started on the right foot. "Is there any possibility that it is Guillain-Barré Syndrome?"

That stopped me in my tracks. "I've not heard of that. What is it?"

"It is a disorder where the body's immune system attacks part of the peripheral nervous system. It normally presents in the legs, not bulbar like Tom's, but it would be worth checking with your neurologist."

Another avenue. "Thanks."

"Regardless, because his breathing test showed chronic respiratory failure," Dr. G. said, "I am recommending immediate BiPAP equipment support to help him breathe. This will also help his muscles rest while he is on the machine."

He made a call to have someone come to the house that day. I was stunned. How could his breathing be this bad and I don't know it? How does this happen? Why didn't Tom tell me? I resolved right then and there to be more observant and mindful of his status every moment that I am with him. Then I thought about the times when I am not with him, working, and started to panic at that thought. What am I going to do?

The BiPAP machine arrived with a wonderful young woman to train us. We sat with our first piece of equipment, which would not be our last. Tom struggled with the machine. He was not comfortable with it at all. He kept saying the settings were wrong.

We had our technician come a few times to adjust it and work with him. Tom knew he needed it, but he objected outright to having any disease that would literally take your breath away.

He had headaches and would be up at all hours of the day and night, without any relief. Our Lyme Literate doctor prescribed oxygen to help him. While that gave him some immediate relief, it caused all kinds of side effects. What we found out from another doctor was that oxygen would be the worst thing for him. You never know when the doctors are right or wrong. Sometimes, you have to go with results and your own decisions.

I started a log to track progress with the machine and to monitor the side effects. The log showed how long he was on the BiPAP each day, headaches, not sleeping, weight, meds, and treatments. It was the beginning of a daily record of the deterioration of Tom and his defiance of it.

1-28-13: BP 11:45 p.m. to 1:00 a.m. Stay up.

Can't sleep BP 3:00 a.m. to 4:30 a.m. Try again, sleep.

2-2-13: No BP—can't tolerate.

Headache a.m. No Benicar. Night sleep not good.

4-9-13: Sleeping with BiPAP 7–10 hours a night. Yeah!

Breathing still labored, need BiPAP. Swallowing, energy and appetite much better!

In the middle of all this trial and error with new equipment, new tough news, and new headaches, a beacon of hope entered our lives. Tom's brother Chris came to visit. His intention was to spend quality time with his brother, which is exactly what he did. He had surmised from the weekly reports that everything was going downhill quickly, and he came to help in any way he could.

Chris was the best medicine Tom could receive. They were like two kids playing hooky from school and living life to the fullest no matter what the doctors had to say. They were both content to watch every sport show and commentary, have their own commentary, blast the music, cook and eat good food and do what brothers do. It was beautiful to watch. Chris not only helped, he was brilliant!

Tom's headaches were becoming debilitating and he blamed it on the BiPAP. I did not know what to do and expressed my concern to Chris. He assessed the situation and said, "Tom, you knucklehead, do you know that you have the BiPAP mask on upside down?"

Tom and I looked at him with astonishment. "What?"

Chris shook his head, smiling. "Yup, I have to come all the way from Florida to teach you guys how to do things. I'm glad I'm here to help!"

"Thank you, Chris. I think you need to stay."

When I looked back on the journal, I was appalled at the roller coaster highs and lows that Tom suffered through that entire year. The log helped to claim accomplishments with celebration and to quietly note the declines. The positives were encouraging to help Tom use the machine. It seemed the log would be the best thing for him if he could get over the physiological thoughts of the BiPAP as a negative instead of a positive.

It took about two months, but finally Tom accepted it to get into a rhythm of life and breathing that was peaceful and calm. Who knew at that time that he would rely on this machine for his life?

February brought us to our Lyme Literate Dr. C to review Tom's status. We were at a stalemate. The aggressive antibiotic treatment for the last six months no longer made any difference. The blood work came back as Lyme positive, but the other strains were gone. We wanted to hang our hat on that result, but we also knew a false positive result was a possibility in this crazy disease called Lyme. It was hard to make sense of it all. Dr. C seemed reticent to give a firm opinion of Tom's status. He said that we had given it a valiant fight.

We discussed our recent meetings with the neurologist and pulmonary doctor, plus our next appointments with the Hospital for Special Care and the Columbia University Medical Center in New York City. Our strategy was to cover whatever ground we could to find the truth.

Dr. C. had heard good things about the Lyme Research Center and wished us the best of luck. All antibiotics were stopped until the Columbia results. This would be our last visit with Dr. C.

I sat there thinking back to the first day we met him, six months earlier. We were positive this doctor would fix everything, so we could get back to our wonderful lives. We were upbeat and optimistic then. Today we sat on the edge of our seats, wondering where this ride would take us. Next was our test and second opinion appointment with Dr. F at the Hospital for Special Care. It was a bright happy day outside, but inside we were not happy at all. It felt like we were walking off the plank of our ship.

The staff greeted us warmly. A dietitian, speech, occupational and physical therapists took turns evaluating Tom. They gave him a breathing test, and we related the history of his illness. They offered helpful advice, as well as telling us what to do and not to do, like Tom was already an ALS patient. This routine established a baseline in order to evaluate the decline every month. If a patient wanted to die here, he could do that, too.

We finally met with Dr. F the specialist, after everyone had reported back to him. He performed an EMG test. The results would determine, in his opinion, if Tom had ALS or not. This is a very subjective test, but the only test available to try to determine a positive diagnosis.

The EMG was an uncomfortable test for Tom. Mini-shocks were applied throughout his muscles to measure how fast the nerves conduct electrical impulses. Then needles were inserted into certain muscles to measure the nerve activity. It takes an hour to perform the entire test. I was uncomfortable just watching what he had to go through.

Dr. F, a very nice, compassionate doctor, had an excellent bedside manner. He looked Tom in the eyes when he delivered the news that yes, he had ALS. He explained the results of the test. We questioned the possibility of Lyme Disease instead; Dr. F said he did not believe it was Lyme.

Tom said, "I hope you are wrong."

Again, looking him in the eyes, Dr. F said, "I hope I'm wrong, too."

It was official. We had a piece of paper that declared a death sentence. It was everything we did not want to believe or accept.

Dr. F described how we would come for checkups every month, or sooner. If we chose to, we could check in there at the end. It sounded too simple. It was a pass or fail life test. We failed.

They signed us up for another set of appointments to check the same disciplines, gave us mountains of paper-work to read and sent us on our way. It was a very dark, gray day outside when we left the hospital for the last time. I commented to Tom how stark the sky and landscape were, compared to when we had gone in. He agreed that it was stark, inside and out.

We did not talk much about the appointment and the results.

We both knew that this was not for us.

There was a snowstorm for our next appointment, which we cancelled; and Tom said he did not want to go back. He did not want to be a number and be treated that way. So I did not reschedule, and they never called.

Our last meeting of hope was two weeks later at the Lyme Research Center at Columbia University Medical Center. This was an evaluation for patients who have "persistent neurologic or neuropsychiatric symptoms that have been attributed to a tick-borne illness." The evaluation would take one day. It would be the same old thing—medical history review, "extensive neurocognitive tests and blood tests," and then evaluated by yet another doctor.

Hope is the thread that holds you together when you are falling apart. Hope can wind itself around you several times like a reassuring hug to make you feel like anything is possible. I had hope that there was a better truth out there than ALS. I needed to have hope to save my Tom, to save us. I knew this was a long shot, but I am a betting girl.

We drove into New York City to find our cozy hotel, so we could rest for our early appointment the next day. Normally, we would have been exploring the streets of New York, enjoying great restaurants, shows, and museums. We tried to go to the French Restaurant downstairs, but Tom thought the food would be too rich for him and wanted to leave. This was his favorite type of food and he couldn't enjoy it. The Irish Pub down the street satisfied our needs with a plain and simple Shepherd's pie that I brought back to the room while he rested.

The next day brought drenching rain with dour clouds and gloomy thoughts. This was not a good sign. The drive to the hospital was a race car track with crazy cab drivers, one-way streets and a world of wet that I traversed my way through. It was a miracle we arrived in one piece. Tom wanted to take the wheel and just drive the damn car himself, but he couldn't.

The hospital was a buzz of activity and foot traffic. When we arrived at our appointment, everything came to a quick, calm quiet. The office was a sanctuary. Dr. D, our angel who had scheduled this appointment, entered right behind us, dripping from umbrella and raincoat. She was a bright spot in our day. She explained what would occur the next two days and encouraged us to relax and ask any questions. Dr. D ironed the creases out of our stiff, worried emotions. She had a way about her that breathed calm and safe.

The next two days, doctors and nurses quizzed Tom and drew blood. They gave him games with cards to assess anything physiological and forms to fill out with Yes, No, or N/A. I was his sentinel to support him as needed.

The initial interviewer asked, "Why are you here, Tom?"

Tom did not blink an eye and said as well as his speech would offer, "I want to know whether I have a final death sentence with ALS."

That set the tone for the day. One of the questions was telling. "Did you ever want to take your own life?"

Tom replied, "Yes, I would find a way to kill myself if I become fully convinced that I have ALS and would undergo a rapid decline. I wouldn't want to burden Jo Ann with that."

I was only able to participate in a small portion of the testing, which involved the drawing of blood. I think they took all the blood he had.

They would call us to consult on the results and send a formal report in six weeks. Our drive home was slow and steady, with positive spirits between the two of us. We hoped for something to help us. We hoped for anything but ALS.

We did not have to wait long for the consult. A conference call was setup to discuss the outcomes with Dr. D and Dr. H, the head of the Center. The lab results showed that Tom still tested positive IgM Western Lyme blot, with three specific bands and eight nonspecific bands. The IgG result detected two bands, which made the result indeterminate, meaning it was on the edge of positive.

Labs performing a Western blot use electricity to separate proteins called antigens into bands. The read-out from the Western blot looks like a bar code. The lab compares the pattern produced by running the test with your blood to a template pattern representing known cases of Lyme Disease. If your blot has bands in the right places, and the right number of bands, it is positive.

The CDC requires five out of ten bands for a positive test result. However, because some bands on the Western blot are more significant than others your doctor may decide you have Lyme Disease even if your Western blot does not have the number of bands or specific bands recommended by the CDC.

Different laboratories use different methods and criteria for interpreting the test, so you can have a positive test result from one lab and a negative test result from another.

The additional testing determined that Tom was negative for Bartonella, Babesia, Ehrilchia and Rickettsia. These results were concurrent with Dr. C's latest test results as well. They also speculated that a positive Lyme result could be a false positive, but the number of bands detected did not lean toward that.

The physiological/physical results were different. Their assessment indicated that Tom was extremely bright but very depressed. They were concerned about his statement:

"Yes, I would take my life," and recommended counseling and perhaps medication to help.

I was eager to understand their opinion on ALS versus Lyme. Their impression and recommendations: "We can neither confirm nor refute this diagnosis of ALS based on the evaluation. However, we would recommend that you look into clinical trials for treatment of ALS. We would also recommend that you pursue neurologic and immunologic consultation in pursuit of additional treatment approaches, possibly with glutamate-modulating agents, for which we have provided referrals."

Post Lab Work Addendum: "The questions are whether Tom is suffering from chronic Lyme symptoms and, if so, whether he would benefit from additional treatment. We recommend that you consider a higher dose of Rocephin, an experimental treatment for ALS, as well as a definitive treatment of Lyme."

They basically said that they saw parallels; and since he tested positive for Lyme with so many bands, there was definitely activity occurring that could seem to be ALS, but there are studies that have proven that Lyme Disease will make ALS worse. Since ALS is not one disease, there are other ways of treating motor neuron diseases.

Dr. H recommended a neurologist in Connecticut who was doing things "outside the box," whom he thought could help us because of our unusual circumstances. Dr. H would contact him, discuss our case, and recommend he see us immediately. Nothing ventured, nothing gained.

The zigzag had brought us through the maze to the other side. It seemed a parched desert. Now what?

I scheduled an escape trip to balmy St. Maarten. We would get away from this life of doctors and stress while leaving the harsh New England winters to make the most of our time together. I had put a hold on my life in every way, except for going to my job and caring for Tom. Painting, blogging my artwork, visiting friends and family, business travel, and social invites became nonessential activities. It was that jog in the road that caused you to turn a sharp left and never look back.

Tom's transition had been slow, but then sped up to fast forward like a bad movie you couldn't turn off happening in the background. His speech, hands crippling, eating, swallowing and breathing evolved in the wrong direction over the days ahead. His mind stood strong.

We needed to get away from the doctors, opinions, and everything except us.

Chapter Fourteen
2013
The Disaster Trip

We can do this.

Perseverance wins the race.

This was not the first time we tried to go to St. Maarten. It wasn't on the official bucket list, but it was where Tom wanted to go. It would be a personal accomplishment for him.

We planned this trip for the first time with our best friends Susan and Doug. We were so excited to escape with them to a tropical isle with Dutch and French persuasions. Everything was booked, Tom's first passport was in the mail, and we counted down the days. We never expected the letter in the mail that arrived—without a passport.

"Passport DENIED." Due to outstanding child support payments. New law, new rules. "You are not allowed to exit the country without full payment of your child support."

Tom had been paying down his child support but still had a balance due. We had no idea there was a new law in place, and we were surprised to find this out five days before our departure. It was a sad day for Tom. He felt like an incompetent dad, person and friend. He just shut down. I was stunned, disappointed and left with the duty to cancel our plans. It was not good. There was nothing good about this.

But goodness prevailed in the end to allow Tom to pay up his child support, obtain his passport and travel out of the country. This was several years later, but under the circumstances, it was a must-do. His choice for an out-of-country trip was still St. Maarten, to conquer a thread of humility and honor. It didn't matter that his health was failing; it mattered that he could do it, because he made it right.

My friend Rosemary had several time-shares that she always offered to her friends, so we accepted her offer and booked a time-share in the Dutch side of St. Maarten. Everything was organized for our departure in two weeks. The planning was fast and furious, with excitement in the air.

I admit, I was concerned about how to travel with Tom in his current state. The airlines were great to offer wheelchair assistance door to door, but I wondered how Tom would be able to move around the island with his shortness of breath and low energy levels.

We had received a bag full of information on the ALS Association, which offered an extensive array of services and help on different fronts. The one thing that stuck in my mind at the time was that it seemed they could help with anything.

The daunting fear of bringing my love to a foreign country in his current state evaporated with this repeat conversation with myself: *Am I doing the right thing? How will I be able to make him comfortable? Is this a crazy thing to do?*

My fears were allayed when I called the local ALS office and spoke to a wonderful woman, the most compassionate person I had spoken to in a long while. I felt like a warm blanket of sunshine enveloped me in positive energy to build my spirit for accomplishing anything. I explained our situation of traveling in three days to St. Maarten and that the Hospital for Special Care had given us their contact information. The calm voice told me they would order a wheelchair and have it drop-shipped to our home in two days. Wow!

She assured me that this trip was absolutely the right thing to do, and it would be the best trip for both of us. If I needed them, they would be available for me long distance. The calm of knowing we were doing the right thing settled over me.

The wheelchair arrived, shiny red and ready to rock 'n' roll. I packed, made sure the passports were in my bag with all the travel paperwork, organized the special food and drinks for Tom, and off we went on our little adventure. My mantra became "We can do this!"

My good friends Rosemary and Deb drove us to the airport. Everyone was excited to make this trip a reality and hopefully bolster Tom into good spirits and health. It was all hands on deck when we arrived to the airport with organized chaos. We chose curbside check-in.

Then it happened—"Jo Ann, your passport is expired." My head almost spun off my head. "What? That can't be."

"Yes, unfortunately, it is expired, which means you cannot depart the country."

This could not be happening to me. "Can I speak to a supervisor? What can I do? You don't understand, my husband in that wheelchair is dying, and this is his bucket list trip. We have to go."

I was crying, hysterical, trying to be coherent, but I couldn't breathe. I kept thinking "I am an idiot, I am an idiot, I am an idiot." Here I am in JFK with my husband in a wheelchair, and I have just won the stupidest person in the world award.

The supervisor came, I tried everything in the book, but rules are rules; and my ability to change them was denied.

My girlfriends had left thinking we were happily on our way, but one babbling phone call from me, and they turned their car around to rescue us. Thank God.

I secretly wondered if this was a sign that we should not go.

As we drove home, everyone tried to calm me down and console me with assurances that everything would be okay. Tom caressed my hand, trying to ease the stress out of me with calm, patient love. He said that when we arrived home we should have a Caribbean party to celebrate our delayed departure and get in the mood.

That's exactly what we did. We drank fruity rum drinks with umbrellas, in our bathing suits, listening to island music blasting, with the heat turned up to keep us warm. A fluffy quilt on the floor became our beach, where we snuggled and whispered sweet love to each other. We imagined the gorgeous sunset fading over the palm trees swaying in the breeze on our own private beach. My guilt evaporated as I basked in this exotic world that we created, with Tom's arms around me.

I finally realized that I was not an idiot, I was just human. A renewed passport took only one day. I changed the plans for a departure two days and hundreds of dollars later for to what we hoped would be a dream vacation. Our actual departure was especially poignant. We had survived a minor disaster, but destiny paved our way to paradise.

St. Maarten did become our tiny paradise. We arrived to tropical temperatures, sunshine and an arid landscape of cactus, not many palm trees or floribunda. I was a little disappointed, because my prior visits to the Caribbean had always been tropical.

The crystal clear, blue waters of the ocean sparkled like smiles welcoming us on the drive from the airport. Our accommodations were perfect, with incredible views. We settled in to rest and recuperate from the trip.

The next day it became apparent that Tom was not well, worse than when we were at home. He was happy to stay in the apartment, watching TV and reading. He didn't want to talk about it. Food was not an option at this point, but I persisted in keeping him hydrated. I made smoothies to keep him filled with some protein. The beach became a non-option, but we managed to enjoy the gorgeous views, balmy winds and tried to have no cares at all.

Our lives came to a screeching halt. Everything else fell away like falling leaves on an autumn day. Nothing mattered except keeping Tom comfortable and caring for him at his pace. This pace was slower than a tortoise in a race to last place. At first, I was fidgety, bouncing off the ceiling of my mind. Then, I started to feel this calm start to take over that felt like the soothing motion of rocking in a rocking chair. I needed to fit into the cadence of our new lives, whatever that was going to be.

I needed to be tranquil and effective at the same time. I started practicing patience by counting while I waited for Tom to drink a new protein shake to see if he could swallow it and if he liked it. I would count to fifty before I asked the next question. I did not want to pressure him. Eventually, I did not have to count; I would simply wait until it was time for the next move. This patience that built inside me changed my person. It made me a better, nicer, happier person because I learned that waiting was not a bad thing; it allowed me to savor every moment. Tom appreciated this new me as well.

There was a wonderful French brasserie and bakery called Bon Appetit within walking distance. I ordered food from them every morning and evening. Tom lived vicariously through me and my visits there to pick up the food.

In the evening, he asked me to go a little early, order a cocktail and learn the local gossip. Talk to the locals and bring back some good conversation, along with the food, for him. Tom would take a taste and leave the rest to me. He was intrigued by the menu, the food and the conversations I had with the chef and bartender when I went to pick up our order; but he could not tolerate food, not even the smell of it. As the days passed, it became worse.

I thought we should go home early to get medical attention, but Tom would have nothing of it. He declared that tomorrow would be another day, and we should go to the French side to see the nude bathers.

That's exactly what we did. I'm not sure if it was the promise of nudity in every size and shape or just the thought of experiencing sublime sunshine and adventures into unknown territory that allowed him to overcome his challenges, but he was brighter, happier than I had seen him all week. I am always amazed at the human ability to put mind over matter.

We set off on our adventure. We maneuvered our way through the island, enjoying the incredible ocean views from every turn. The little towns we passed through oozed with European charm, from the decorative doors, shutters and colors, to the ornate railings and livestock roaming the land. Everyone on the island appeared to be carefree and happy. It was contagious.

We managed to find Orient Beach, parked the car and wheelchaired to the first tiki bar. A drink was in order, even if there was only one sip. Mango sours were the special of the day. After getting our bearings, we were directed to the section of the beach that had service, comfortable recliners and umbrellas. Tom decided the wheelchair could be left behind.

A waiter approached us. "Bonjour, how can I help you?"

"We would love a bottle of champagne, with two ham and cheese crepes."

"Oui, but of course."

Our food and drink arrived while we sat back and watched the parade of humans, scantily clad or buff and bronzed on every square inch of their exceptional bodies. The surf in the background framed the scene with delightful energy and color. Our conversation reverted to who was pretty, too fat, and too skinny. Of course, there were perfect people everywhere.

Tom asked me to walk to the end of the all-nude beach. I would be his eyes. He was too weak to walk himself, but he wanted me to see it for us.

It was a bizarre scene. Most people there strutted their stuff, totally clean shaven, looking amazingly bald. They did not seem as beautiful as the people on our beach; it was showtime for them.

Tom was eager for the report and enjoyed all the unusual details immensely. He fit into the landscape like it was made for him. French persuasion, beautiful people, and heavenly weather took the weight of the world off his shoulders. He was finally able to relax and just be who he was, without illness or fears.

It was a delightful afternoon, worth its weight in gold. This day told me that even though the entire trip was tough for Tom, he would not have given this up for anything. He was happy. I did the right thing.

The following day brought us home and back to reality.

3-6-15

Dear Tom,

    It struck me one day when I was sitting at the beach looking at these old couples that I would never have what they had. I would never grow old with the love of my life. I would never wither and dry up, sitting on the beach with my love. Those old couples sit on the beach as some of the wisest creatures on earth. They have no wants or needs except to sit in the sun, soak up the rays and hold hands. I wonder if they still have sex. I think so.

    I wish it could have been us.

Love you, darling.

Chapter Fifteen
2013

The Transition

Could it be true?

IN MARCH, THERE WAS NO TIME FOR THINKING. As soon as we returned, Tom was hit by a whopper gout attack in his wrist and toe. He could hardly move without wincing. His pain was so loud I could hear it across the room. Gout resides in his family history, with his grandmother Mimi and his brother Chris the targets of this painful affliction.

Tom's prior diet of rich foods, red meat, seafood, mushrooms and scotch were a sure way of causing a gout attack. A daily dose of Allopurinol had been his first defense. That had worked well, unless he was excessively indulgent. But now, his diet consisted of nothing on the bad list of gout makers. He did not deserve gout on a painful plate filled with all the other medical situations.

I immediately called Dr. A, his primary care doctor, and explained the situation. I expected no cooperation, due to our last communications, but he immediately prescribed Prednisone to battle this monster.

Thank you, God.

The Prednisone not only alleviated the gout symptoms, but Tom's breathing improved, and his appetite and energy levels improved significantly. We knew this was a miracle drug for gout attacks, and it was now Tom's "Get Out of Illness Jail Free" card. We dined, danced and declared a Gout Out Holiday to make the most of the time we had until the script ran out. We captured a little bit of our old life in the center of fighting for our lives. It was wonderful and humbling.

My attention finally turned to locating the "outside the box" neurologist that had been recommended to us at the Lyme Research Center. My research found a man with many credentials and specializations, including Lyme Disease. I called to make an appointment, but the first one was three months away.

There was nothing I could say or do to make it sooner. I asked for any cancellations and wrote an email to Dr. H at Columbia University Medical Center, the Director at the Lyme Research Center, to request his help. He replied the same day that he had called Dr. J (the third neurologist) and that I should call for an appointment within the next two weeks. The power of networking was alive and well.

When I called, I was greeted with expectation and warmth. Dr. J would see us in six days. Hallelujah!

The transition started as life calmed down and we waited for our next challenge from fate to occur.

All we had to do was live our life to the fullest every day and try to not think about what might be.

I was concerned that because no one could understand his speech, Tom was becoming a hermit, not wanting to engage with his friends. More research, and I found a text-to-talk app for him. He loved it. There are a lot of simple to extravagant devices on the market that can allow a speech disabled person to communicate with the world and feel part of it. I'm not sure why this didn't dawn on me earlier, but he was ecstatic to have his voice back. He became very proficient with a stylus held between his thumb and forefinger to type in words so that he could talk. He was like a two-year-old learning to talk for the first time and able to have a real conversation instead of just listening to the noise that surrounded him.

My favorite was, "You are the most beautiful woman in the world inside and out." He made me feel beautiful.

He also had a great sense of humor. He typed in another saying when I got home from work after one very trying day when I wanted to pull my hair out. "All work, no wine, what's a girl to do?"

His favorite phrases:

"Could it be true?"

"I think it's time for bed."

"Shut the front door."

"There, of course, is a method to the madness. Cook the White Castles per box instructions, then take out of package, open the lid and top with relish and mayo, wrap in paper towel and cook for twenty seconds."

"Flag on the play."

"That was the most sumptuous orgasmic meal you have ever made for me. Thank you!"

"Good Job, Honey!"

"All this and no PC, what's a guy to do?"

"So many choices, woe is me."

"Sweet dreams."

This app allowed him to interact with people again and be in the limelight. His personality and humor picked up where he left off, not skipping a beat, and everyone enjoyed it immensely. Tom was able to receive guests or go out and about with the ability to communicate and be a human being again.

Our friends and family had the opportunity to visit Tom and spend time with him, which was extremely precious. These new social activities helped my mental health, as well as Tom's. We always loved to entertain, and now Tom could feel comfortable spending time with other people. It was a gift for everyone.

His fingers were crippled, and it was hard for him to hold utensils or pens to do the *New York Times* crossword puzzle, but he found a way. Eventually he stopped doing the crosswords. He said it was too hard to write. I offered to write for him and he could teach me how to do crosswords. He replied that I could never learn to do crosswords and he was done with them. I tried not to cry when he told me. He was not emotional about it; he accepted it without fanfare. I don't know if I could have given up something that I loved as much as he loved his crosswords so easily. It was extremely sad. How could I change this sadness?

One day slid to the next without any yellow lights to slow them down.

He asked me to go shopping for him to get new clothes in smaller sizes. I thought that he liked the baggy, comfy look, but was glad to go shopping anytime, so that was not a problem. I bought him new jeans, shirts, underwear, belt. He was at his twenty-one-year-old weight, seventy-five pounds lighter, feeling like he looked great, and he did. The first forty pounds, he tried to lose; the rest came off by itself.

In my mind, it was a toss-up whether the weight loss was from ALS or Lyme Disease. Lyme antibiotic treatment can reduce your appetite substantially, but ALS causes your system to become "hypermetabolic," burning calories at a faster rate than normal.

Couple this with difficulties swallowing, and that automatically leads to weight loss. Tom had become a fashion horse, thanks to my influence in our early years. He loved to be color coordinated and fashionable.

Then one day he asked me to go shopping for clothes without buttons or snaps. He was not able to button his clothes for himself and did not like the idea of being incapable. I did go shopping again and had to return everything because the sizes were too big. He was losing weight at a faster pace than I could keep up with.

There was a time that he used to make lunch for me every day, when I came home from work. He was not able to do this anymore. Then I worried about him coming down the stairs in the morning and getting the oatmeal that he made for himself every day. So, we changed our schedule to get him up before I went to work, to get downstairs, settled and reading the *New York Times*.

He made his own oatmeal and enjoyed getting up and walking around a bit, but then that changed, too. His legs started to give out under him, and he could not walk on his own. He still wanted to walk, with me giving support by offering him one arm while he walked, but it was not easy for him. He had an inner strength to be resolute, strong and in charge of himself, as much as he possibly could.

We needed to see Dr. J, and the miracles he could make for us.

Chapter Sixteen
2013
The Referral

"This Lyme versus ALS is a very tricky situation..."

SOMETIMES THE ODDS ARE AGAINST YOU, SOME-
times they are in your pocket.

Our first appointment with neurologist Dr. J in April was
a game changer. We expected nothing. The initial appointment was not covered by insurance, but we decided it was
worth the investment. Luckily, one of our guardian angels
sent a gift of the exact amount required, which was unexpected and humbling.

We received a welcome package that explained the process, cost, and other information. It explained that Dr. J
used his dogs for his patient's benefit and, "If you do not
like dogs, find another doctor." At least we knew that we
were dealing with someone with strong opinions.

We were buzzed into the office, which was small and
decorated like a sitting room in someone's home. There
was a large framed print of John Lennon with the lyrics to
"Imagine" printed on it. Tom was a big John Lennon fan and
automatically felt comfortable with John hanging out with
him. Other various paintings of good taste captured our

interest as we sat alone and waited to be greeted. It was a room without a view, without people, without sound.

All of a sudden there was a pitter-patter of feet, the door flew open and three adorable dogs on leashes flew into the room, excited to see us. They had good manners and just hovered at our feet, waiting to be petted and appreciated. The master behind the leashes welcomed us and apologized for the delay.

"Good Morning, I am Dr. J and you must be Tom and Jo Ann? So sorry for my lateness, but duty called. Thank you for coming. Let me introduce you to Rincky, Maggie and Lizzy."

They were quite a motley crew, definitely in charge, with a Shar Pei–Beagle mix, Boston Terrier and an English Bull-dog. Adorable.

"Good morning, it is a pleasure to meet you." It was as if we were dinner guests in his home.

"Please follow me to my office down this hall."

The dogs followed and settled around Dr. J's desk, except for Maggie, who hopped up onto her special chair. I would find out during the initial interview that Maggie was also an artist. She would create spring art by chewing pens and getting the springs out to mesh together in different contortions. Dr. J had them displayed on his desk. They were actually quite good. His office was ornate with large paintings and two wood framed plush chairs in front of a huge wooden desk covered with books, papers, equipment, and an assortment of knickknacks. Obviously, these gifts and collectibles were important to him.

He sat down in his leather chair behind the desk and asked, "How can I help you?" His dark brown eyes held a sincerity that made you feel like you might live forever under his gaze.

I started to speak, but he wanted to hear from Tom first.

Tom explained, "I have been diagnosed with ALS and Lyme. I want to know if I'm going to die and if you can help me."

It was not easy for him to deliver this message with his current speech, but he persisted, and Dr. J was patient and understanding. Dr. J related that he wanted to hear his speech for himself.

I then handed over the stack of documents from the beginning of Tom's illness, with a three-page timeline detailing what had occurred so far, along with all the supporting documents.

Dr. J asked for time to absorb everything. As if on cue, the dogs ambled over to occupy our attention. They were comforting to have around, instant stress relievers.

Dr. J's head popped up. "I'm extremely sorry that you are not well. I think I can help you. This Lyme versus ALS is a very tricky situation, but after reading your records and reports, I believe that there is a significant finding in your testing that indicates that you could have MMN—Multifocal Motor Neuropathy. The EMG report clearly states that there is a conduction block which indicates that it is possibly not ALS.

"The treatment is intravenous immunoglobulin, IVIG. This is a long-term treatment that can be successful, but it is extremely expensive, and the insurance companies do not like to approve it. I need additional testing to confirm and justify to the insurance companies the treatment is required. In the meantime, I would like to try using immune factors. This is experimental, but I have accomplished 300 procedures over the last three years with no side effects. This could improve your symptoms."

We sat there in silence, letting this news soak into our brains, our hearts and our souls. This was certainly "outside of the box medicine," but that is what we needed.

We spent three hours with Dr. J, reviewing all the data, discussing the details, trying to understand if this new potential diagnosis could be true. He also performed a physical exam. More blood work was ordered, along with a Prednisone taper 5, which Dr. A, his family practitioner had not done, plus several additional supplements and scripts that could help Tom. We would come back after three weeks, when the taper was completed, for the first immune factor treatment, which was a diagnostic to learn more details of what was happening inside Tom's central nervous system. We felt we were in good hands for the first time.

On our drive home, Tom typed on his text-to-talk app. "Could it be true?" He played that for everyone and anyone. It became his mantra.

As the Prednisone tapered, so did Tom. He became extremely fatigued; speech, breathing and swallowing became more difficult every day. Weight floated off his body onto mine. We mutely chose to ignore these declines and silently hoped that Dr. J would work his magic on Tom to solve the riddle and save the day.

It was only three weeks. We could be patient and make the most of this precious time.

Chapter Seventeen
April 2013
The First Treatment

Gremlins . . .

EXPERIMENTS WERE MADE TO CREATE CHANGE IN the world. We hoped this experiment would change our world for the better.

We arrived on a Sunday morning after our routine of coffee, newspaper reading and the forties music, making us feel as if nothing was wrong.

The dogs greeted us warmly, and Dr. J was excited to begin.

He reviewed the blood work results and was sorry to advise us that MMN was ruled out due to lack of GMI protein levels. This was not good news at all, but he explained that this was a process of ruling out with investigative testing to solve the puzzle. The good news was that Tom tested negative for Hemochromatosis.

We moved into the exam room and Tom sat on the cold steel covered with paper. There was another picture of John Lennon. This brought Tom to speak his best in a long while.

"I was in New York City when Lennon was shot, Doc."

Dr. J stopped what he was doing, enthralled. "What was it like? Where were you? How was everyone around you?"

He wanted to know everything. They talked back and forth about that night while everything was prepared for the procedure. It was as if they had been friends forever.

Dr. J explained that this would be an injection, like a spinal tap. He would anesthetize the area, remove spinal fluid for diagnostic test and then inject the immunoglobulin directly into Tom's central nervous system. Dr. J was shocked that no other doctor had performed a spinal tap diagnostic test. This would allow him to try to understand what caused his symptoms, as well as substantiate IVIG treatment in the future.

We were banking everything on this procedure, on this day.

When I saw the size of the needle, I closed my eyes and said a silent prayer that we would both survive this. Tom of course was as strong as strong can be. He took it like the man that he is. He wanted to live.

Then we took our first roller coaster ride. Dr. J had warned that there might be some side effects, and that within two to three days, Tom should start to feel better. He was right.

That night and the next day brought head and neck pain with waves of nausea and something close to a migraine with light causing him severe pain. He also had a low hum and pressure in his right ear. We called these immunoglobins gremlins. Tom could feel those gremlins doing dastardly things to the bad cells in his system. He wanted the war inside him to win this battle, even though he was suffering.

Everything eased up the following day, and on the third day it was gone. What replaced the side effects was better speech, an appetite, ability to walk freely without the wheelchair for short distances and a huge smile on his face. Unbelievable! Could it be true?

The new regime of additional meds and supplements grew to ten items. The medicine cabinet was open for business.

One month later, holding our breath, we returned for the spinal tap test results.

Dr. J expressed enthusiasm and hope. He did not make us wait long for the verdict. "Tom, you have an extremely rare result. Your spinal fluid shows Oligoclonal Bands, which indicate inflammation in the central nervous system compartment. The lab report states:

"'The patient's CSF contains five well-defined gamma restriction bands that are also present in the patient's corresponding serum sample, but some bands in the CSF are more prominent. This pattern is associated with Guillain-Barré's syndrome, peripheral neuropathy or increased permeability of the blood-brain barrier secondary to infection or trauma. This is a Demyelinating Disease—Oligoclonal Bands & Demyelinating Disease.'"

We had it in black and white. It was not ALS. Dr. J advised that he needed a Spinal MRI and IVIG treatment immediately. He would send in this report with a request for insurance approval. Meanwhile, he would continue with immune transfer treatment, since it showed great improvement. He could not give a definitive diagnosis without the additional testing, but with this report, he believed that it was not ALS.

It was time to not only celebrate, rejoice and pinch ourselves to make sure it was real. It was time to savor every ounce of life that we could possibly swallow.

Chapter Eighteen
June 2013
The Power of Positive

Majestic palms lined the highway . . .

THINGS WERE LOOKING UP. TOM WAS ENERGETIC, alert. He wanted to do what he couldn't have possibly done two months ago.

His brother Chris was graduating from Police Academy, and Tom decided that he could not miss it. So, we quickly arranged a trip to the Keys to celebrate Chris's graduation. He was excited to see his brother, his sister Jenny, and Chris's family.

It was the best thing we could have done. A change of scenery, with paradise surrounding us from every angle, would make anyone feel better. It wasn't just the scenery or temperatures. It was hope.

I was still a little paranoid about this pronouncement of health and brought all the paraphernalia, meds, equipment and protein drink supplies to take care of an army, just in case. I needed to be prepared for anything and everything.

Our trusty red wheelchair gave Tom the premiere drive through the airport. Tom argued that we did not need it, but I insisted. "Honey, we are bringing the wheelchair. You can push me if you feel strong enough. Just enjoy the ride and save your energy for me."

He smiled boyishly. "If you insist, my love."

The drive down the Florida Turnpike with the music blasting was just like the first time we drove it together so many moons ago. Majestic palm trees lined the highway, standing at attention with their branches saluting us as we passed by. The sun shone bright and beautiful wishing us a hearty welcome. The air tasted of blue skies and toasted sagebrush with fires burning far off. We felt like VIP's in this world away from what we left behind.

When we came to the bottom of the turnpike, a sharp turn left brought us onto Card Sound Road, one of the two ways to enter or leave the Florida Keys. This shortcut gave us the glory of huge, magnificent Crocodile Lake out of nowhere, then to Alabama Jacks. It was one of our favorites, a stop half-way down the road in the middle of nowhere, with great food and sassy staff. Entertainment did not include music, but the mangroves captured the flight of birds, while crocodiles floated in the waterway next to our table as we dined. Extra cold beers and plump steamed shrimp in old bay seasoning, and a split blackened grilled dolphin sandwich, rounded out the experience to know you were in the Keys.

As soon as we left, there was an adorable one-dollar toll booth, stuck in time. We enjoyed a fun chat with the toll man, since there was no traffic, and then followed the straight and narrow road for twenty miles of nothing, except lush mangroves and waterways. Suddenly, there was water on both sides of the highway, reflecting the sunshine with ripples of laughter and charm, welcoming us.

There is nothing like driving down Route 1 with water surrounding you in all its colorful glory. There are so many colors in the water; you can't count them on your fingers. Close your eyes and they will all be different. Squint your eyes and the color sharpens the values to Day-Glo, capturing the essence of the Keys.

Then you feel something decadent, dreamy and invisible creeping into you, like a silent wish, making you feel at one with the air, the water and the road. Delightful. As we drove down that highway with the windows down and the air rampaging through every sense, pushing and pulling my hair everywhere, I could feel and see the worry we both held so tightly just float out the windows.

It floated over the bridge into Crocodile Lake and was gobbled by the crocs.

This is what we needed to pacify our fears and fill us with hope for better things ahead.

The graduation was dress right dress in military format, with Chris leading the way. Tom and I were so proud of this veteran who fought for us overseas, fulfilling his dreams of becoming a police officer and working to keep peace here in the USA. The celebration of life continued with cheers and tears of happiness.

Of course, Tom supervised the graduation party food prep—with his culinary expertise—that Chris, Jenny and I prepared. He immensely enjoyed doling out directions with his text-to-talk phone.

"Add coffee to the BBQ sauce for some chutzpah!"

We captured all our hearts together that night.

Tom was at his best throughout the celebrations, but when we were together alone, I could see how he dwindled down to half a pulse. He allowed everyone to see him at his best, and I allowed him to be himself with me. It worked. We worked together.

It was a great trip that made Tom feel more complete. It's funny how things that you thought would make you happy, like a bucket list, pass by unnoticed, then you figure out what the real deal is. Spending time with family made us the happiest. The touch, the laughter, the looks and the feelings of love do more for the soul than anything else. Chris and Jessica, his wife, and their two children, Aubrey and Colin, wrapped their arms around us and never wanted to let go. It was hard to leave, not knowing when we would see each other again.

We traveled home with dread of what would be next. We had departed on our trip with great news but could not ignore how the balloon was deflating at the end of our stay.

1-4-16

Dear Tom,

If only you were here in person, but you and your spirit are certainly with me this morning. We didn't have a chance to stop on our last trip for Chris's graduation, but our memories are still here. I'm at one of our favorite breakfast places in the Keys, Midway Cafe. The name is so appropriate since it is midway between Miami and Key West. As always, when you walk in the door there is a bustling atmosphere of half-asleep people waiting patiently with eyelids almost open, while the staff is bright-eyed and bushy-tailed with big smiles and wake up exuberance. The hum in the wildly decorated back rooms where everyone enjoys their meal is lyrical and pleasant with whiffs of coffee, cinnamon and toast. It is as if you are in someone's warm and cozy home that is decorated just to make you happy with different bright colors at every turn. One table has writing that says, Keep your lives free from the love of money, be content with what you have. So true.

I decided to sit outside in the cool, 67-degree shade just outside the main entry and watch it all from afar.

As you know, the menu is extensive with yummy delectable baked goods or breakfast any way you could imagine it, which always gave me pause for what to order. But today I do not delay and know exactly what I want. I place my order at the front counter where a sign proclaims, <u>Be nice or leave.</u> That sign says something so profound in such a soft, sweet way that you cannot help but be extra nice. We should broadcast it on social media, TV, radio and the airwaves every single day all over the world. Maybe the world would not be in the state that it is today. So, I order an egg sandwich, eggs over-easy, bacon, and Cheddar cheese on a croissant. They deliver it to me with a smile and an oversized mug of delicious coffee.

I take a bite of my sandwich and the yolk pops out and runs all the way down my arm, slowly, sexually, and soothingly warm. This is a perfectly cooked egg...maybe you are helping in the kitchen? I don't even flinch because I know it is you. I want to savor the feeling of your touch and your embrace of me. But, reality clicks in and I must lick it off with total enjoyment. If only you were here, my love. We would wrap our meal to go and find somewhere to finish the deed. I love you and miss you, my love. I will be back to Midway Cafe when I'm in the Keys and always savor the memories of you, their fabulous food and infectious smiles.

Love, Jo Ann

The Beat Goes On

Tom picked out a romantic B&B...

IT WAS TIME TO SEE DR. J.

Tom's health had improved immensely, but after six weeks without an Immune Factor treatment, and traveling, he was going downhill quickly.

Dr. J greeted us warmly and wanted to hear all about our trip and the tropical Keys. He shared with us his love for the tropics, and how he wished he had more time to spend there. Then we got down to business. Standard evaluations of lung capacity at thirty-seven percent and ALS score 33/39 determined that Tom was stable. Dr. J noted that Tom's weight was declining, down fifty pounds since January. Immune Factor or IVIG every three weeks was necessary to maintain his stability and stamina so that he did not become a jackrabbit, jumping high, then low.

The insurance company had not responded yet for the IVIG approval, which would make the treatment easier at home. This treatment is extremely expensive and requires an in-home nurse to administrate it. Nothing is easy.

Tom was still receiving speech and occupational therapy. He was encouraged, but I did not see any difference, except for his positive attitude about getting out and communicating with people.

Little red dots entered the scene, all over Tom's arms and legs. Dr. J indicated that it could be (ITP) Idiopathic Thrombocytopenic Purpura. We needed to make an appointment with a hematologist. It was time to get out of Dodge and try to find some sanity.

The Fourth of July was the following week. Mimi had wanted us to come out for our traditional holiday visit, but Tom hadn't been able, until now. We waited the requisite two days of IF (immune factor) hangover as we called it, and Tom felt fit as a fiddle can get.

"Honey, I want to go visit Mimi for the Fourth of July."

I was surprised. "Why the hell not, Mimi will be thrilled, let's do it!" This will be good for Tom.

The idea of going to Cleveland and seeing all those fabulous fireworks 360 degrees around Mimi's building made me think of a long-forgotten memory of my childhood.

I was a kid roaming the neighborhood with the neighborhood clan, consisting of my brother, my cousins and friends who played together. I was the youngest. It was the Fourth of July and the air exploded with firecrackers all around us. Our merry band went around being mischievous, setting off firecrackers and having fun. Fireworks were illegal, and we had made a lot of noise with them that day, getting ready for the big fireworks display that night.

My cousin Sharon, who was the oldest of the group, said, "We have to have an escape plan if the cops come down the road."

I said, "We can just lie down on the grass and pretend we are green grass."

They all laughed at me, saying I was so young and silly. At that moment, a cop car started toward us. Everyone scattered in every direction, except for me. I just plopped myself down flat on the grass, with an entire string of fire-crackers in my hand, and closed my eyes. I felt a shadow cross my space, blocking the warm sun.

I heard a deep voice. "Hello, are you okay?"

I opened my eyes to see a giant officer in uniform with a big brimmed hat and a gun in his holster. I was a little scared and wasn't sure what to say but decided to stick with my plan. "Hi, I'm fine. I'm just pretending to be grass."

"Are those firecrackers in your hand helping you pretend?"

"Yes, sir."

"Why do you have firecrackers?"

This was not going to be an easy answer, but I had to think fast. "Oh, they help to protect me. I am too young to light them, but they are strong enough to protect me from the bugs when I pretend to be grass."

The officer gave a small smile and asked, "Where do you live?" I pointed in the direction and told him my name and street, which was around the corner of the next street. It was a time when everyone knew everyone, and kids roam-ing the neighborhood by themselves were normal and expected.

"Would you like a ride home?"

"No thank you, I'm just gonna be grass for a while."

"Well, if you are sure you are okay. And you are not going to light those firecrackers by yourself, I guess you can enjoy the rest of your day."

I felt like I could breathe again. He left with a small smile on his face, off to find some real crime. I realized that day in my young six years of age that anything was possible.

I have to get back to this feeling again. That anything is possible.

Again, I packed expertly everything we needed, including all of Tom's paraphernalia, meds and muck. I felt like a drill sergeant moving out the platoon. Of course, I packed our special red, white and blue flag shirts to wear for this special occasion. When we called Mimi to tell her, she squealed like a little girl, so delighted that we were coming.

We decided to stop halfway overnight in Pennsylvania, since it was eight hours to Cleveland. Tom had picked out a special romantic B&B for us. It was almost as if there was nothing wrong. We checked in and found our cozy room. I moved everything inside and looked for the BiPAP machine. I went back to the car three times. It was not there. I could not find it. I had left it behind!

I couldn't breathe at that moment. Tom could not go the weekend without his machine. He needed it to endure. Tears started rolling down my face. What to do?

I dried my eyes, went back to the room and told Tom that I screwed up and left the BiPAP behind, somehow. He was shocked and upset. That was his lifeline. He didn't have to say the words, I heard them loud and clear . . . *How could you?*

There were two options. Go home without going to Cleveland. Or I would do a roundtrip home and back to the B&B that night. He thought I was crazy to drive that distance alone, but I had no choice; I screwed up. So, after getting food and meds set with Tom, I departed into the night.

It was only an eight-hour roundtrip, with lots of coffee, good music and singing at the top of my lungs. Tom stayed awake and we talked now and then. It was almost like when we were first dating, when he would call, and we would talk into the wee hours of the night. It was a good thing I could understand his Tomese language, with his trademark slur.

He felt bad that I went, I felt bad that I had left the machine at home, and we both felt bad together, making it something good. Something called love.

At first sight of Mimi, Tom's energy soared; just being in her presence was enough. She had difficulty understanding Tom's new language, especially with her diminished hearing, but I translated for her and soon we found a rhythm together. This short time was exactly what Tom and Mimi needed to feel better. Mimi was a hundred-one-and-a-half years old, looking great, and Tom's medical age was close to hers. Being together brought their youth back to them; it was quite miraculous. They built each other up and made the world shine brighter.

Friends and family came from near and far to see us while we were there. No one knew when or if they would ever see us again. Cocktails with friends who lived in the building was entertaining and uplifting for us. It was how life used to be. My daughter, Jennifer, and her family drove three hours from Michigan to spend a day with us.

This was a special treat since we didn't see each other very often, just talked on the phone a lot, much more than we had when I first divorced. I am very proud to call my two kids my friends. When you grow up and have your own children, it gives you a different perspective on life and how hard it can be sometimes. I adore my grandchildren and luckily, they adore me, too.

We grabbed every moment we could have together and stuffed the memories into our pockets like smiles that we could keep forever.

We visited the Cleveland Museum of Art, taking turns pushing Tom around in his red wheelchair. He loved having the children, Esther and Elijah, cater to his every whim and constantly press their love on him at every chance. Beautiful.

Positive attitude is an amazing thing. Tom and I could have been dour and negative during this visit, but everyone's love, coupled with our positive attitudes, changed Tom's physical and mental status.

His speech seemed to improve. His swallowing was better. Magically, he had an appetite again and was able to eat a normal meal. This was a first in six months.

Mimi's request for dinner was fried chicken and potato salad, with Tom's favorite dessert: cherry pie with ice cream. Quintessential Fourth of July fare was perfect. Her wish was my command. We dined overlooking the sublime skyline of Cleveland, with fireworks and camaraderie entertaining us throughout the evening. The bursts of color and electricity created an energy that recharged our batteries. The fireworks on the Fourth contributed to the fanfare and were the best and last that we would see in Cleveland with Mimi, but they would never be forgotten.

The ride home was long and quiet, draining our batteries while we recalled all the special nuances of this wonderful trip. Then we started to think about what waited for us when we arrived home. If we kept driving, maybe we wouldn't have to go back to the reality of our fight for survival.

We returned to more doctor appointments that seemed like a bouncing ball we were following to nowhere. Tom and I established a status quo: Tom's breathing was controlled by BiPAP use both day and night now, instead of just nighttime. The devilish red dots diminished on their own miraculously.

It seemed his swallowing improved, because he could drink more, but swallowing was not easy. Soft foods helped him obtain sustenance. He claimed that his energy improved, but not to the extent that he could do anything more than he was already doing, which was not much.

His hands were stronger and could do more things, but chef work was out of the question. Speech was a daily challenge that seemed to change daily from better or worse like a yo-yo.

The list of meds reached nine total, some twice a day.

Details of the diminishing man continued to be logged.

It was hard to make sense of it all.

Our next appointment was with Dr. K, the hematologist. His diagnosis, after more blood work, was Hemochromatosis. That is an iron disorder in which the body simply loads too much iron. This action is genetic and the excess iron, if left untreated, can damage joints, organs, the brain, and eventually be fatal. Tom would now have to endure four sessions of phlebotomy, a procedure to take blood out of the body, thereby thinning the blood. Known in more primitive times as bloodletting, it was often done with the use of leeches. Regular phlebotomy treats people who have too much iron in their blood, such as those with Hemochromatosis. (Evidence points to Ernest Hemingway having inherited this condition, and passed it on to his children, resulting in the high rate of suicide for three generations, including Hemingway himself.

After that, Dr. K wanted to perform a bone marrow biopsy to determine what was causing the unusual WBC and RBC counts. We also received a referral to see a rheumatologist, who might be able to help Tom with his unique circumstances.

How much more could we take? How much more could he endure?

Our last appointment of the month, or so we thought, was with Dr. J for a checkup and IF treatment. The pattern of treatment was becoming routine. Dr. J, concerned about Tom's WBC and lymphocytes, ordered a chest X-ray. Another visit to another medical office, for good reason.

The X-ray results showed linear opacities due to atelectasis in his left lung. The antibiotic was changed to help the situation, and I was instructed to change the BiPAP filter/hose/facemask and sanitize everything to eliminate bacteria. I had thought I was doing this, but I needed to do a better job to eliminate any possibility.

How do you fight the ghosts of bacteria and know that you have won?

But there was one more doctor's office visit, to the rheumatologist, Dr. L, without good results. Dr. L was pleasant enough, but it became obvious that I knew more than he did. I gave him Tom's history and asked him questions pertaining to it, and he had no answers. He didn't seem to know what I was talking about.

Dumbfounded does not even describe how I felt. There was no need for wasting everyone's time, so I shook his hand, thanked him for his time and said we were leaving. Tom's smile told me that he agreed wholeheartedly.

Our month of doctors and diagnoses, or lack thereof, ended with us celebrating surviving it all. Tom was tired and not his best, I was exhausted, trying to keep up with work, home, doctors, bills, research, and maintaining Tom's regime. But we were alive and kicking to make the most of it and were glad that we were here to complain about it all together. The anchor was dragging us through the mud.

Chapter Twenty
August 2013

The Traffic Jam

Tom put on his grumpy pants . . .

THE STARS WERE ALIGNED FOR A CRASH COURSE.
Tom seemed to be crashing and burning all at once. The positive signs in Cleveland flew out the window, replaced with my notes in the journal of "not good," "still not good, BiPAP day and night," "leg muscles very weak due to condition, phlebotomy and new antibiotic," "HBC/RBC all up," "stopped antibiotic, felt better," "not a good day, breathing is extremely bad today, exhausted, high humidity and temps outside."

Something had to change.

We had been seeing Dr. J for four months and had all our trust in him. The insurance company had not yet approved his request for IVIG, since May, and we did not know when it would be approved. This treatment was our last hope. I called the insurance company and wrote a letter. Dr. J wrote letters, but we could not obtain a definitive answer. They did not care that someone was dying while they went through the bureaucratic nonsense.

I could not sit still and wait forever, so I went back to my research to look at other options for neuromuscular disorders. My sights were set on Massachusetts General in Boston, John Hopkins in Baltimore, a specialist in Colorado, and Penn Neuroscience Center in Philadelphia.

I didn't have to make the decision; it was predestined.

Tom's cousin Danny called to schedule a visit with Tom. He joined us for lunch. Tom had been very particular about what he wanted me to prepare for lunch. Chicken salad, with tarragon, almonds and grapes on a bed of greens. The food was still important. His lunch was a protein shake, but he could taste the salad with the accolades from Danny.

Danny was glad to see Tom and did not mask his surprise at how he looked. Tom communicated with his text to talk, which gave Danny a mixture of surprise and admiration for his innovation and perseverance. They railed against the current sports and shared family gossip while enjoying being in each other's company.

We finally started talking about Tom's health status. I related where we were and how I felt we were stuck in the mud and needed to branch out and obtain other help. I showed Danny my sheet of researched places to contact.

He raised his eyebrows. "Jo Ann, I know someone at Mass General I think could help you and Tom. He is one of my clients." Predestiny was at work.

"Danny, how? Who?" Could this be true? I expected many hours of phone calls, letters and waiting, waiting and more waiting.

Danny replied, "Let me make some calls, I will be in touch."

He left us smiling and full of hope, grateful for his contribution to our crusade.

We didn't have to wait long. Danny called that afternoon to say he had made contact with someone who had contacted another, and they communicated with the head of Neurology, who was on vacation at the Cape. She would see us in ten days at Mass General. Miracles do happen! Danny followed up with an email of introduction and contact information. The power of networking at its best, saving lives, one at a time.

I'm not sure what we expected. But doing something was better than doing nothing.

The head of Neurology was a prominent doctor in this field and had significant expertise on the subject of ALS and Neurological Diseases. She gave talks on different subjects that you could call in to listen, as well as ask questions. I immediately signed up and avidly listened. She spoke in down-to-earth terms while specifying the medical details. It was like going to church when they spoke in Latin, but you understood everything that they said. The one statement that stood in my mind was "ALS is not one disease." She went on to explain the different types of ALS that had been defined. Autoimmune was one of them, same as Lyme Disease.

With fingers crossed and a Hail Mary, I made the reservations.

The next day, Dr. J called personally to inform us that finally the IVIG was approved! It only took four months. The first treatment would be conducted in his office in five days. After that, a nurse would come to our home every week, or every two weeks, for the treatments.

Everything was happening at the same time. The stars were aligned for positive results, one way or another. I just hoped they did not crash.

Everyone was in good spirits when we arrived at Dr. J's office. This was happening! The atmosphere was as jubilant as New Year's Eve at midnight. We could have brought an appetizer and a bottle of champagne to celebrate. Dr. J was especially excited. He wanted to perform the first procedure under his supervision, to make sure that Tom accepted it without problems before it was administered at home.

A series of premeds was included, to help with the side effects and impact to the system. IVIG is administered intravenously; it took approximately two hours. Two quiet, hopeful hours that felt like a lifetime. I could not imagine how Tom felt, taking all this in and wondering if it would work for him. Could this be it?

This was our lucky uneventful day, except mission accomplished! The next treatment would be in four days, right before our appointment at Mass General.

The IVIG medicine was hand delivered to our house the day before, in a large package with huge ice packs, to keep it cold. Everything needed to be stored in refrigerator immediately. It took up half the space. I now needed to get a wine fridge. They also delivered a mountain of medical equipment and supplies. I thought we were done with that, but we were now open for IVIG business. Half the dining room became the storeroom. It was almost like a pizza delivery service, but the opportunity of life was being delivered instead.

The doorbell rang promptly at nine the next morning. I opened the door to a smiling, tall, beautiful, blonde woman with the happiest eyes I had seen in a long time. "Hi, I'm Jane, your new nurse."

"Hello Jane, welcome to our home."

Jane was immediately attentive to Tom. I could see him open up to her and feel her charm, as well as her happiness showering on him. It was like watching a closed flower bud open slowly and shine brightly. Of course, Tom's charm for a pretty girl perked him up like nothing else. I could breathe, relieved. I could see this would be the perfect tonic for him. The IVIG treatment might help, too. That was our hope.

The side effects were minor, with a headache, tingly feet, and intermittent sharp pains here and there, but ibuprofen took care of that. Tom did feel stronger in his legs, his breathing improved, and his attitude was positive that this might help him. He slept well, knowing there were good guys in him working to kill the bad guys. He needed his rest for the next day's trip to Mass General.

Tom put on his grumpy pants for the drive to Boston. He was not sure why we needed to go to another hospital to be poked and prodded just to be told that he had ALS. I disagreed. Perhaps they had new technologies, and Dr. M stated in the podcast I had listened to that ALS is not one disease. Maybe, just maybe, they can help understand the relationship between Lyme Disease and ALS? Yes, he would be put under a magnifying glass to check every gorgeous ounce of him, but that was a small price for the miracle I hoped for.

As we drove into Beantown, the stately buildings seemed to be guards at the door waiting for us, greeting us with a truly Bostonian highbrow wave. We said thank you for the $15 billion Big Dig completion, to get us to our destination effortlessly. The hospital had supplied a list of accommodations close by with reduced rates.

We splurged and stayed at the Liberty Hotel which was an original historic jail. Ironic that we wanted freedom but stayed in a jail. Tom was still a little grumpy, tired, and most likely apprehensive about our appointment the next day, so we settled in for a nap and room service. The city buzzed around us with opportunities, but we were content in our luxurious cell to just be in our own space together.

The next morning brought bright sunshine, the promise of anything positive, and Tom's cousin Cal, who lives outside of Boston, works in Boston, and knows Mass General inside out, due to his own medical battles. He was our guide and savior, maneuvering us through the crazy maze of corridors to our destination.

Tom's cousins surrounded him with love and a spirit of "yes, you can conquer this, and we will help you." Everything was always upbeat and positive, even if the writing was on the wall.

Cal and Tom shared more, since they were both fighting for their lives, but looked at life with those rose-colored glasses. It was beautiful to watch them together. The talk was about sports, family and friends. Compassion simply melted between them like the chill of a warm cozy sweater on a crisp cold morning.

Cal was diagnosed with Chronic Lymphocytic Leukemia (CLL). He fought it and won the battle with the help of his brother Danny, through a bone marrow transplant and arduous treatments. Above all, his determination to live brought him through. I am happy to report that at this writing, Cal is two years cancer-free, living life large and one of the happiest people I know. He rubbed off on Tom for good luck.

We reported for duty, my expectations high, Tom's unknown.

Dr. N, a resident, was assigned to us to accomplish the initial evaluation. It was as Tom expected, poking, prodding, questions and then do it again. Tom was seen by four different people doing their jobs, asking their questions, testing all parts of him. Dr. N was wonderful to stay with us through it all and answer any questions we had. They did a thorough job of evaluating his status, to advise Dr. M, Head of Neurology.

Tom was not happy. "I told you this is how it would be."

He was right, but I still felt this was the right thing to do. "I know, honey, but we will be done soon and then we will meet Cal for lunch."

As we sat waiting to see Dr. M I wondered what I would say, and how this person could possibly help us. I was as exhausted as Tom, but I could not show it, feel it or even think about it. I used my own personal pink umbrella to repel the negative thoughts away from us.

Dr. M entered the small room where we waited. She was tall, well groomed, and had the eyes of a saint. She reminded me of Julia Child, with both her stature and reputation. I hoped that Tom felt that, too, which would have calmed him, since Julia was his idol.

"Good morning, Doctor." I introduced ourselves and we settled down to talk.

Dr. M started the conversation. "It is a pleasure to meet both of you. I have reviewed the details of Tom's medical records and of our review this morning, and I am so sorry for your diagnosis of ALS."

I had to jump in. "Doctor, we are here today because we are not convinced the diagnosis of ALS is correct. As you can see from Tom's history, this all started with a tick bite, Erlichiosis, then all the versions of Lyme Disease one could possibly have. The actual ALS testing showed a conductive block, which is contrary to a definitive conclusion. Further, Tom has just started IVIG treatments that are having a positive effect. We had scheduled this appointment because the IVIG had not been approved by the insurance company, and we were desperate for another opinion. I am extremely impressed with your accomplishments in this arena and know that you feel that ALS is not one disease. Is it possible that it is not ALS?"

The air in the room stood still, with the hairs on my arms standing at attention, waiting to hear something that I could swallow.

"Jo Ann, forgive me. You are correct, ALS is not one disease. Tom, I will restate my apology. I am sorry that you have a Neuromuscular Disease. Your history has two highly unusual contributors to your status. Lyme Disease is an autoimmune disease that can certainly contribute. The other puzzling piece is your history of gout and high uric acid in your system. ALS patients never have gout, and we actually give them uric acid to slow down the Demyelinating process or the shutting down of the nervous system, which has been effective. I am curious to see your antibody report, which could indicate what study might work for you. We have an immune suppression study scheduled in three months and are also looking at stem cell treatments in the future. Also, there is a genetic study on the C9ORF72 chromosome 9 that is one year away that could have a significant impact."

My mind was spinning. I could only wonder if we had another year. It felt like we were in the hub of a technology landscape that could break through the barriers and find a cure for whatever disease we wanted to call this, but would it be in time for Tom?

"We have many studies that have helped patients in the past. We are always learning and finding new treatments to solve this puzzle. Meanwhile, it is important for you to take care of yourself and receive periodic medical reviews. I would also suggest genetic counseling. We will be happy to do that for you."

Tom sat quietly watching the debate over him, center stage, from the sidelines.

"Doctor, what is your opinion on IVIG for Tom's situation?" I asked.

She smiled warmly. "You should certainly continue it, especially if you are seeing positive results. Tom, your disease is unique and will probably continue its decline. I hope the IVIG treatment is successful for you."

Tom looked up and smiled. "I do, too."

"Not Good,
I Feel Like I Am Dying."

We were trying to win this battle together...

OUR LIFE CHANGED. WE SETTLED INTO A ROU-
tine of daily optimism that changed like the weather
reports. We had no need to go anywhere or do anything,
except for my work and the monthly visit to Dr. J or Dr. K
for a phlebotomy. This schedule was easy compared to the
chaotic revolving door of doctors, testing and trips in the
past six months.

Life centered in our home, with weekly visits from Jane
for IVIG, plus visiting nurse therapists, and infrequent
friends and family dropping by. But mostly, it was just us. It
was the most precious time in my memory. It was also the
scariest time. New changes in Tom echoed Dr. M's words
of doom; that if he was not young, and the stem cell treatments started too late in the disease, he would continue to
decline. But the IVIG did help.

One week, his speech, strength, appetite and swallowing would improve; the following week he would experience swallowing, walking and breathing difficulties. His

hands became more crippled, his mouth had a twisted, droopy smile when he did smile, but his eyes held all the warmth of an apple pie just out of the oven. He didn't care that these things were happening to him. He just cared that I was with him and we were trying to win the battle together. He was the best soldier.

The fall walked past us without notice.

My various notes created a pattern of Tom's declining health, but I did not want to see it.

"Not good, I feel like I am dying," Labor Day.

Lost 100 pounds—started Calorie Counter to gain weight.

First day of Sunday Football—makes Tom very happy, especially when his team wins.

Phlegm is our new enemy.

Treatment number seven, Jane said Tom's speech and breathing is much improved—no hangover—Happy Anniversary to us!

Tom slept eleven hours last night, arms and legs tired and heavy today.

Decidedly better breathing all day, not labored at all. Mom and Dad came for an early Thanksgiving dinner; Tom loved Mom's pumpkin pie.

Up two pounds . . . yeah!

Very weak today, could not stand well. Red dots on feet that are swollen.

Rough day, not eating well due to swallowing. . . found oatmeal, miracle food for Tom.

"Feels like I'm going backward."

NOT a good day, very quiet today.

Cannot eat anything, only water, changed IVIG to ten-day schedule with hydration first. Pedialyte to the rescue.

Hydration by Jane, works wonders.

Up four pounds, feeling "Fit as a fiddle" today. Took a ride to get out of the house.

Phlebotomy crash and burn night—stop the treatment, please.

Phlegm city, change diet to no dairy or lactose, cough assist and nebulizer added.

"Please cancel appointment with Dr. J, I feel it is pointless." No, we are going.

Feeling okay today, three days in a row.

Great Day for Tom besides being my birthday, excellent speech and energy. We even danced a little, yeah!

Not a good day or night, not eating or drinking, nausea and phlegm.

11:30 p.m. trip to Emergency Room for breathing. Wanted to admit, declined

Albuterol is our new wonder drug.

Lots, lots, lots of phlegm, don't know how to stop it, not eating enough.

Down ten pounds.

Got Netflix today, Tom in good spirits.

Good News, Dr. J reported test results show the degrada-
tion of the disease has stopped from pre- to post-IVIG.

Thank You for everything you do. I couldn't do it without you. I love you Tom

This last day of the year report was supposed to be positive, but it felt like it did not matter. Nothing mattered except trying to keep Tom out of harm's way every day.

The holidays slid by without any *fa la las* or merriment. The bright spot was an early Christmas visit from my son, Bill, his wife, Tara, and our granddaughter, JoJo. She was three years old and at the height of her curiosity about Santa Claus. We tried to see him right down the street, but he was out feeding his reindeer. Instead, JoJo and I decorated our home to make us "happy." There is nothing like young excited children to brighten your day and make you feel loved. Tom's smiles spoke loudly.

Chapter Twenty-Two
January 2014
The Last Trip

What are you scheming now?

I WAS GETTING CABIN FEVER. THE MONOTONY OF the ups and downs of this disease, combined with the cold winters of New England, called for a change. It was like a bugle in my ear when I was sleeping one night: *We need to go away, to somewhere warm, sooner than later.*

Predestination is my best friend. I had given up posting on my Painting A Day blog a long time ago, but I followed several artists who impressed me by their work. One particular artist had a very unusual style of painting in oils that was fun, vibrant and inviting. I had signed up for one of her workshops but had to cancel due to Tom's illness. Tom kept encouraging me to paint, to attend her workshop, but I could not see how that would be possible under the circumstances.

But today, being the first day of the year, after that bugle blasted my fuzzy brain clear, anything was possible. I jumped out of bed, fired up my computer and went to work.

Before Tom woke, I had found that the same artist was having a workshop in Marco Island, Florida in eighteen days, and she had an opening. I called Jenny and Chris, Tom's siblings—could they come to Marco Island to be with Tom while I attended the workshop? They said yes! They were thrilled to be able to see Tom and spend time with him.

I found a beautiful four-bedroom, handicap-equipped home with an in-ground pool on the Intracoastal Waterway. Perfect! He always loved adventure. Direct flights were available.

I sat patiently waiting for Tom to wake up to say yes, while bursting at the seams with excitement. This was too good to be true.

He woke, pattered down to the kitchen, made his oatmeal, and settled down to the Sunday paper, with forties music playing in the background. Before he could dive in, I made my move.

"Good morning, darling, how are you feeling this morning?"

"Good morning, my love, I'm really not sure how I feel yet, it's too soon."

He was still fuzzy. And I felt like I had just climbed Mount Kilimanjaro with the exhilaration of accomplishment.

"How do you think you would feel, waking up in Florida with sunshine and warm weather instead of these gray skies, chilly temperatures and dour forecasts?"

That grabbed his attention. "What are you scheming now?"

"I woke up with cabin fever today," I began, "and I thought you might be feeling the same way. This ride we are on needs a new point of view. So, I did a little research this morning. That painting workshop you've been urging me to take is happening in Marco Island, Florida, on the West Coast. They have an opening. Chris and family will come up from the Keys and Jenny will come as well. It will be great to have your family with you while I paint. I found a gorgeous house you will love. We should go for the week. What do you think, my love?"

He had an amused curl to his lips while he entered his text-to-talk response: "Darling, when you put it that way, how could I refuse? When would we go?"

Yes, Yes, Yes!

"Well, we need to get Dr. J's approval, which I don't think will be a problem, then we would be there in eighteen days. How's that for fast and wonderful?"

The curl turned into a big gigantic smile. "Honey, you are the best, thank you. I love you."

"Honey, I love you, too. It will be great for everyone." Everything was booked within the hour, and we had something positive to look forward to. The bonus came when I told my daughter, Jennifer.

"Mom, I can't believe this, we are going to be in the vicinity, visiting Greg's grandmother at the same time. We can come visit you! It would be absolutely wonderful to see both of you."

I knew they were going to Florida but didn't know when. Amazing!

Excitement reigned for the next two weeks, which helped keep Tom's health normalized so we could make this trip. The packing was precarious, with all the extra meds, equipment and Tom's special foods, but I managed to do my best and organize everything, double checking and making sure we had the BiPAP machine, first and last. That would never happen to me again.

The travel was easy, with assistance from the airline, to whisk us through security on both sides to enter paradise.

As we drove over the bridge to Marco Island, our oasis was freeze-framed in my brain—heaven on earth. The receiving line of palm trees, with the ocean sparkling in the background, gave the feeling of relief and sanctuary from whatever anyone suffered from. This was a place where we could be happy for a little while and forget.

The island welcomed us as if we were its dearest friends and nothing was wrong, everything was right. If only that could be true.

We found our house, giddy to be here in this place, at this time. It is amazing what a change of scenery will do. Tom, ever quiet lately, became abuzz with conversation and excitement. His text-to-talk skills were razor sharp.

"Wow, I love this place. When will Jenny arrive? I'm hungry, what can I eat? When does your first class start?"

"Honey, I love it, too. It is exciting to be here with you. Let's make every moment count. It will be special."

This week in paradise will stay in my memory bank as the best week ever. I have had incredible weeks in my life, but this one spoke to me in a different way than all the others. This week captured what it was to love someone and share someone with all the other people he loves, too, and for them to share his love. It was a love fest. Love in a way that makes you feel like you will always be loved, no matter what happens next. True love.

This was the best thing we could have ever done. Lots of pictures were taken, but the most poignant picture was of Tom and me standing outside our house with our grandchildren, Esther and Elijah. I had my arm wrapped around him, which almost circled his waist, covered by his blue Key West T-shirt. The kids were boisterous and we all managed a halfway smile. Tom was all there, except for his eyes; they were tired and vacant.

It was the first time I had seen this, and it scared the living daylights out of me.

5-24-15

Dear Tom,

It's Sunday morning. I was lying in bed thinking about lots of things like what I was going to do today, who I was going to see, who I was not going to see and random thoughts of work, friends, family, places and of course my thoughts always came back to you.

I was remembering how cozy and safe it was to be in bed with you. I especially loved Sunday mornings when we were able to sleep in and laze dreamily together. I can still feel the warmth of your skin when your arms and legs were wrapped around me like a love knot. We would just be in each other's space feeling like we were the happiest people on earth that we had each other.

Sometimes we didn't even have to say "I love you" to each other because it was said in a different language, a language of touch. Sometimes now I can wrap my arms around myself in a way that it feels like your arms holding me every so gently and lovingly that I'm sure you are there if I closed my eyes.

I know you are there and I feel you every day.

Thank you.

Please never leave me.

Chapter Twenty-Three
2014
Stem Cell

He always celebrated this day . . .

I'M NOT ACTUALLY SURE HOW IT OCCURRED. WE were going along day by day, dealing with everything we had to deal with. IVIG treatment continued, but Tom's health eroded on fast-forward no matter what we did. I was intent on making him as comfortable as he could be and keeping a positive attitude for him and for me.

He was declining in front of my eyes, even though I told myself it could not be true. I could accept everything as is, forever, as long as he would not suffer and would not die. Anything would be better than losing him forever. But, if I thought about it from his perspective, he most likely would not want to continue to live this kind of life forever. It would not be living a real life, just coexisting on the end of a string with the threads revolving out of reach.

Every night we had our routine. We would watch certain shows like *Jeopardy!*, the *Nightly News* with Tom Brokaw, and whatever show he had recorded, maybe *American Idol* or *Glee* or *A Chef's Life*. One of the shows he watched relentlessly was *Snapped,* which I could never watch because it was too scary for me. I would have nightmares if I saw anything with blood and guts in it. I always said he was plotting to kill me, and he would laugh.

It occurred to me that Tom had become obsessed with death and how people died. He became fascinated with the *Nightly News.* We all know that the news seldom gives us good news; it is always fraught with people dying from murder, war, or horrific diseases. I'm not sure if this was because of his depression, or if he was just getting himself in this state of mind, the mind of death.

He knew he was going to die soon, but he didn't want to acknowledge that reality to me. Watching these shows gave him the opportunity to be with his kin, in a way.

He was always a night owl, staying up to all hours watching movies, TV, or listening to music. I would try to keep up, but I had my own necessary routine of sleep and early rise, to go to work. I would typically fall asleep on the couch, and when he was ready, his text to talk would say, "Honey, I think it's time for bed."

The ritual for nighttime was for me to walk him up the stairs, help him into the bathroom, help him to brush his teeth, change his clothes and get him into bed. We went from dry mouth, that required a certain rinse, to wet mouth with too much phlegm, that required different items to help minimize it. I had to move the BiPAP upstairs, change the water and disinfect the machine, but the chores were nothing compared to keeping him comfortable and safe.

When we were both in bed, his text to talk would say, "Good night Honey, I love you," and I would say, "I love you, sweet dreams." We would hug and hold each other until we fell asleep.

One night, he could not make it up the stairs, his legs were too weak. No problem. We would sleep downstairs on the couches. Fortunately, our couches are very comfortable, and they made perfect beds.

I ran upstairs and found two quilts, sheets and our pillows to make our beds downstairs in the living room. It was important to me to make this a normal situation, like nothing different was happening, except that we both knew that was not true. We went through our same rituals, but in different places. I found a bell that I rigged next to Tom's couch, for him to ring in the night if he needed to get up.

The next day, I went to the store to obtain a portable urinal, so he would not have to get up in the night to use his energy walking to the bathroom. He always wanted to walk on his own, with only the help of my arm and me by his side, in case he could not make it. His dignity shone brightly every single time he did this.

I was scared and most likely he was, too, but there was no show of fear whatsoever. It was as if we were on our own little island of love and contentment with each other, where reality could not touch us. I knew that I was losing him one day at a time. I didn't know what to do except to love him, be at his side for better or worse and to try to keep our spirits from sinking. I would not show my fear either.

I persevered to make it better. I made phone calls to see if I could arrange for an electric chair for the stairs. The CT ALS Association again came through and connected me with someone who could offer me a chair lift at a substantial discount. I arranged for him to come to the house to measure the stairs and see the setup.

Life was different for the next two weeks. We slept downstairs every night in our little oasis of love. I would be home more than at work. I knew his sleep schedule, so I would slip out to go to the office, which was only five minutes away, and do what I needed to do there, then I would go home and work remotely as necessary.

I was extremely fortunate to work for a firm that cares about me and understands the priorities of life. I have an amazing staff that handled things while I was not all there in body or mind.

April brought the opening day of baseball. This was a rite of passage for Tom. He always celebrated this day by shaving off his beard in honor of spring and baseball season. Seventeen years in a row, he went to the Yankees' opening day in the Bronx with his friend. Not this year. This day, he was going for his first stem cell treatment with Dr. J and Dr. O from India, who had successfully treated patients for various illness with stem cells.

We had waited for this day a long time. I was excited about this treatment. Since I am always the optimist, I hoped and prayed this would be the magic treatment to save my precious Tom.

The morning of the appointment I found Tom sullen and sad. I asked him, "What's happening?"

"I'm not excited about this and don't think it will make a difference."

I was too quick to respond. "How do you know? I thought we wanted to try this to see if it could make a difference? Are you scared?"

He barely whispered, "I don't know."

I think I was the only person who could understand what he was saying at this point. It was a different language, but I understood it clearly. I also wanted him to continue talking to make him feel as normal as possible.

"I know that I'm scared. I have never been more scared in my whole life for you. We are in this together, even if you are doing all the hard stuff. We don't have to go. I can call and cancel right now."

"No. We'll go."

"Are you sure?"

"Yes, let's do this."

I'm not sure if he agreed to go for himself, me or us, but he decided to go. He was the strong man in the circus, the champ of all the teams everywhere and my hero.

Then I remembered opening day. I went upstairs and found some of Tom's Cubs' paraphernalia, including hat, jacket, and an official Cubs shirt. I brought them down and he rewarded me with a bright, happy smile.

I took a picture of him in Dr. J's office in full Cubs attire. He looked worn, tired, depleted, and thin, but he had that look in his eyes and that smile on his face that said, *You have made me happy. I love you.*

This was the first stem cell treatment in these offices. We were fortunate enough to be on the top of the list with our wonderful Dr. J, and Dr. O who came all the way from India. Tom felt dehydrated and asked if he could have an IV before the treatment. He felt his batteries were low and needed some recharge before the big event.

There were two patients in the office that day. The other patient went first, even though Tom was supposed to be Dr. J's first stem cell patient. They flipped a coin. Tom called heads; tails won the toss.

The luck of the draw can make a difference between life and death. The first patient did not have a successful process. He panicked and started hyperventilating, which did not allow him to continue. The procedure was aborted, and an ambulance came to take him to the hospital, to make sure he was stable.

We were in the next room hearing this happening in muffled sound. I would pop out into the hallway to hear better and report back to Tom. It was agony sitting there, hearing anguish. Then it was over. We heard the emergency call go out and saw the medical team arrive with a gurney, the reality of the situation front and center. I was afraid for Tom and what might happen to him.

Shortly after, the hospital reported that the first patient was resting comfortably and was okay. Dr. J wanted to call it for the day, since it was not a good start.

Tom disagreed. He wanted to proceed. Can you imagine the courage that one man can have to walk into a situation that might end him up in the hospital, or worse? I know we both had total faith in Dr. J and we also had our hope that this could do something to save Tom. It could save his life.

After much discussion, it was agreed to proceed. I had brought Tom's BiPAP, since he seemed to need it more now than ever. I knew this was going to be an anxious time that could directly affect his breathing. It was the best thing I could have done. The BiPAP calmed him down by allowing him to breathe freely and put him in a place that made him seemingly invincible.

They asked me if I wanted to watch. I declined, since the last time I participated in an intrathecal procedure, I fainted at the sight of the needle.

Tom's favorite nurse, Mandi, would assist. Mandi and Tom were like peanut butter and jelly, the sweet and the gooey. She was always there for him, helping in a way that only a good nurse can. Tom loved her attention to him and how beautiful and fun she was. They always joked with each other. As they were prepping for the procedure, music surrounded everyone with wistful promise of good things.

Tom talked through me about dancing to this song one day. "This is a perfect song for dancing."

I agreed. "Mandi, Tom is the best dancer ever. If you ever have a chance, he will whisk you off your feet and you will never be the same."

Mandi smiled and said, "I could only imagine how wonderful it would be to dance with you, Tom."

His smile was ear to ear, with his boyish charm. "It would be my pleasure; we have a date."

They had a very special relationship which made her the perfect person to assist this critical procedure. Tom had total confidence in both Mandi and Dr. J. I sat in the next room during the procedure, saying my prayers.

Tom survived the treatment, with the help of his BiPAP machine to keep him breathing easily. Everyone celebrated the accomplishment and could not compliment Tom enough on his courage and stamina to get through this tough procedure. I took pictures of Tom with the doctors and his favorite nurse to commemorate this momentous day.

When we waited for the stem cells to return to Tom's system via IV after harvesting, I had the opportunity to talk to Dr. O. He said this treatment was more effective on younger patients in the earlier stages of a disease. What he didn't say was that Tom was too old at fifty-five and too far in his disease, but the message was clear.

I know that Tom did this for himself, but I also think he did it more for me, even if there was only a small margin of potential for lifesaving results. This could be a way to extend our lives together and allow him to live. I also know that he did it for mankind and all the other people out there dealing with a disease that does not have a cure. He gave it up to try to find a cure. He was the bravest person I have ever known.

It was an exhausting day. We went home back to our little cocoon downstairs to coexist in this world called ours. The expectations were that he would feel worse, then better in five days.

He had two days of better, then he seemed worse than ever. His breathing worsened, he could hardly swallow, and he was so tired and weak.

It is true that stem cells work in your body trying to fight the bad cells and rule the world. It is like chemo, except it does not work the same way. It either works, or it doesn't. It didn't for Tom. I didn't know what to do. I called Dr. J and asked if he should have Prednisone, or more IVIG. What to do? I did not have to wait long. A series of events brought us to our next crossroad.

Chapter Twenty-Four
Easter Will Never Be the Same

I was afraid to tell Tom . . .

IT WAS EASTER WEEKEND, BUT IT DID NOT FEEL like Easter. My family had a traditional Easter breakfast that was command attendance when my grandmother was alive, and I was a little girl. The tradition included church in the morning and then a breakfast, with Italian Easter breakfast foods homemade the two days prior. This special family gathering has continued every year since she passed away many, many years ago.

The menu was the same every year, including pizza gain (Italian meat and cheese pie), anginettes (puffy citrus cookies with pastel frosting and sprinkles), pepper bread (made from pizza dough, Crisco and lots of black pepper), ricotta cheese pie, (sweet ricotta cheese with sugar, eggs and a delicate lattice crust), Italian cheeses and meats and shots of whiskey to wash it down. (A tradition from my grandfather.)

Since the family has grown, we have split the menu and responsibilities amongst everyone, including an Easter egg hunt for the kids. It is a perfect time to see everyone in the family and spend time with wonderful, memorable food.

This Easter breakfast would be without Tom and me . . . a first.

My dad's health had been waning for a long time, but since he is in the *Guinness World Records* for the most heart procedures of anyone I know, it seemed like just another health problem that he would solve and go on. He always took great care of himself, eating the right things, trying to exercise and be healthy. We always talked about what diet we were on, how much weight we had lost, and what great healthy recipe or food we just found. He was an avid gardener, fisherman and hunter. Over the years, he has had to give up his large gardens in the yard, due to his health, but his green thumb still ruled his deck, with his vegetables and flowers. My dad was my hero from the day I was born to the day he died. He had a passion for life, love of everything and everyone, and the best attitude one could have. He gave me so much.

My job for Easter breakfast was to make pizza gain— delicious and full of calories. My grandmother made the original recipe, and we have five different recipes from the five sons' wives in our family cookbook. Of course, I always made my mother's, which in my opinion was the best.

I made the pizza gain and brought it to my mom and dad's the day before Easter. When I walked through the door, the scents of Easter filled my heavy heart with brighter memories of days gone by. The Easter lilies eased some of my pain, while the undeniable pizza in the oven drew me into the kitchen. I half-expected to see my grandmother at the stove cutting up the rectangle pizza into squares. There was leftover pizza from Good Friday, with the extra pizza dough from baking for Easter, which was another of our traditions.

Dad seemed too quiet and not in good form. I asked what was going on. He said he was very tired. He had gone fishing that morning for opening day. He had not gone fishing in a very long time, due to his health, but this special opening day of fishing found Dad out there with his daughter, Debbie, and his grandson, Louis (his namesake). He told me that he thought he might have done too much, but it was the best thing he could have ever done. It felt good and right. He was happy.

I was concerned about his pallor and breathing and urged him to call the doctor. He said he would on Monday. I asked him to promise or I would call. He promised.

Easter Day was a blank page for me. The artist in the sky washed the canvas clean and declared that someday it would be again. I did not feel like anything was possible. I wondered how other people in similar situations got through it all. How did people continue to take one step at a time forward with the world crashing in on them like a dark black hole? I realized that people did overcome worst possible things, and I could too.

Dad went to the doctor Monday morning, and they rushed him to the hospital by ambulance. He had a bad case of pneumonia. They started treatment immediately and said he would be there a couple of days and would be fine. He died the next morning without any of us there.

I will never forget when Mom called saying that Dad was in distress in the hospital and doctors said it was time for the family to come right away. I was at work, in a meeting. I dropped everything and left immediately. I could not fathom that my strong, tough dad could be in trouble. He had been through countless heart procedures, near-death events, and lots of medical situations before, but this felt different.

I called to make arrangements for someone to be with Tom while I went to the hospital. Susan dropped everything and was there to help Tom, thank goodness.

As I entered the hospital, I knew that all was not right. When I got to his floor, my three sisters and my nephew James greeted me outside the ICU doors. It seemed like a slow-motion movie. I looked at my sisters and saw something in their eyes. James took my arm and walked me into ICU. He said that Poppi, as he called my dad, did not make it. It was surreal and crazy.

"James, what are you talking about? Of course, he is okay. Where is he?"

"Aunt Jo Ann, he died . . ."

"Oh, my God, how is that possible? He was going to be okay."

"I don't know, but it is true."

It was an impossible reality. He died without all of us, without any warning or expectations. It seemed unreal until I saw him. It was true that he died, but he was not gone from us and never would be. The fact that he was still warm when we got there made all the difference to me. We did not get to say goodbye or be there with him when he left this earth, but his warmth was something he left behind for us to feel his love for us. It was his way of waiting for his family. It seemed that he was still with us, and then he turned cold as if his spirit left.

I had never been this close to death. I had never imagined Tom dying from his disease, but now it was a stark reality.

We all stayed at the hospital with Dad for a few hours. We cried, we screamed, we hugged Dad and touched his face; we held his hand and told him how much we loved him and how much we were going to miss him. We held each other and tried to help the pain. It was painful and beautiful at the same time.

Mom had just had dinner with him in the hospital the night before. Not being with him when he passed was brutally painful for her. They were planning their fiftieth wedding anniversary in June.

I came to realize that he saved Mom from suffering his death, because he was the strongest one of all. He decided to spare us the horror and complexities of being there when he died.

After a few hours, it was time to leave the hospital. Mom was in shock and needed to be in a better place. I corralled all of us to go home. We did it hesitantly. We did not want to leave him but knew we needed to. We stopped by the nurses' station and thanked them for everything they did for our dad. We did have an opportunity to talk to one of his doctors, who was very compassionate. He informed us of everything that happened and seemed very upset about losing him.

This was impossible. It was unimaginable that my hero was gone. He was never ever going to be gone. Why? Why now when I needed him to be here to help me? And we did not get to say goodbye. This was not gradual; this was unexpected, shocking and horrible. I felt like my insides were ripped out with the shock of it all, but then I realized that he died in a good place without drama and pain.

We walked out with heavy hearts to leave our dad. When we went downstairs into the lobby, I saw a shiny dime on the floor and picked it up. When we went out the front doors, there was another dime. I took Mom to drive with me and we went to the parking garage. There was another dime on the way.

I told Mom that these were dimes from Dad. When I was a teenager, he always asked if I had a dime in my pocket to call him if I needed a ride. These dimes were his message that he will always be there for me and us.

After standing still in the dark waters of death, everything changed to a whirlwind. Family and friends descended on Mom and Dad's home. Food, flowers and wishes came pouring in. We had to make arrangements. I needed to take care of Tom but could not leave my family. Thank God, Susan was in charge at home and taking very good care of Tom. I talked to both of them and would be home after everything was taken care of.

I was afraid to tell Tom. I did not know how this would affect him in his precarious state, but he needed to know. He had a special relationship with my dad and was very concerned about him. Tom took the news astonishing well, or so it seemed. But he was in shock, too.

Mom was not in any shape to make decisions and asked me to take care of everything. I was the eldest and needed to take charge. How would we do this? I had three younger sisters here and an older brother in Florida in a nursing home. I had been to a lot of funerals in my life, and in our family, there was a particular format everyone followed. Should we do something different? Follow the norm?

My first memory of death was when my first mom died, I was only ten.

I am very lucky to have had two moms. My birth mom had separated from my dad. I lived with her, and my brother lived with my dad. She lived life to the fullest and was my role model for my life, then and now.

My dad remarried, and my new stepmother eventually became my second-best mom. I couldn't ask for better.

When my first mom died, I remember going to the funeral home and seeing her in an elaborate box with flowers and pictures all around. I remember everyone looking at me and whispering about me. I knew that she was not there; she was in my heart and always would be. I did not cry. I did not feel anything. I didn't know what I was supposed to feel.

This was different. This funeral was for Dad, so it needed to be the way he would want it. Our family is very Italian, which meant that church and ceremony are very important for our family and for Dad's memory. My dad did not go to church every week, but he sent us to parochial school to be raised "properly." The nuns and the Church did contribute to shape me into the person I am today. I enjoyed that until high school, when I asked my father to please transfer me to the public school system, so I could see more boys and be with my friends. He was happy to oblige since it would save him money and make me happy.

My three sisters, Debbie, Susan, Karen and I went to the funeral home to make arrangements. We did this without knowing anyone's wishes. We made the decisions and had a beautiful and sad two days of wake, plus a full funeral Mass, burial and traditional Italian luncheon. My dad had touched many, many people's lives. and they all loved him. An overwhelming number of people came and expressed their love and admiration for him. I was so proud to be his daughter.

Tom could not come to the wake but was adamant that he would attend the funeral. I know now that this pulled every ounce of strength that he had because of his health and his fragile state of mind. He loved my dad and felt a large loss in his life. It was hard for him to accept that my father was really gone.

We sat in the church during Mass and I cried like a schoolgirl who had lost her best friend. I think I also cried for Tom in his wheelchair, and my brother Michael in his wheelchair, mourning a great man they both admired and felt close to. Crying can be contagious, and you need lots of tissues. Tom started crying and asked me for a tissue. I looked and could not find one, so I gave him one of my dad's handkerchiefs. He thanked me and then I told him it was Dad's.

"Great, now you're killing me." He whispered that in my ear; only I could interpret it.

The entire family came in from all parts of the country. It comforted me having my daughter and son with their families holding us up. Over the years, my daughter and son had come to love Tom and appreciate how happy he made their mother. They always stayed on the sidelines of our lives, like an audience watching a movie they could be part of. Their acceptance of Tom and me back into their lives filled my pocket of loneliness with love. My daughter was there for me in so many ways. My son fell into the same category in the way only a son could.

I saw Tom sitting there in his wheelchair as someone I loved and hoped would never have to go through any of this again. He sat as a shrunken shell of what he used to be in girth and stature, but he was a statue of strength that powered over me, even though his suit drooped over his bones as if it was in mourning, too. The scarf I had wrapped around his neck to keep the chill off his bones captured his tears.

I felt his pain, which was so much more than mine.

It felt like we were on the edge of the end.

That night, when we came home from the funeral, Tom said he wanted to talk to me. He text-talked that he loved my dad very much and was so sad he was gone. He said that the funeral was beautiful, but he did not want that kind of service when he left this world.

"What would you like instead?"

He said, "A celebration of my life with my music and TK coffees for everyone." This is the epitome of Tom. He is the eternal hippie and coolest soul on the planet.

"Would you like somewhere special? Is there somewhere you have in mind?"

"No, you decide." Then Tom added, "I want to be cremated and my ashes to be cast in the waters of Key West behind Hog's Breath Saloon."

"Of course, I will, my love, and when I die, my ashes will go right next to yours. I will also take you with me in my travels to be with me always."

"Thank you, I love you."

"I love you." We sat and held each other to hold us together before we broke into a million pieces of sadness.

10/24/14

Dear Tom,

It has been hard for me to get back to writing . . . four days have gone by and I am stuck in the muck of my mind. I have made up one excuse or another to not sit down and write. I'm not sure why, but I think it is because now I will start writing about the tougher times. Every day going forward in my memories will be harder for me, as they were for you. This is why I have put them away in a very safe filing cabinet in my brain. I have locked them, but now I need to find the key. That key has a capital C on it which stands for Courage. I have to remember that I had the courage to live it and I need to cherish it now. I know I can do this. You know, too.

Love, Me

Chapter Twenty-Five

Fourteen Days of Nothing Normal

My brain was spinning . . .

AFTER MY FATHER'S FUNERAL, OUR DAYS TRIED to go back to normal, but there was nothing normal about them. Tom declined at a rapid rate. His breathing had worsened, his phlegm a constant problem. He had aspirated once; it was extremely scary to see how he struggled and I was afraid that he would not be able to breathe.

I did not know what to do except to follow the prescribed course of treatments. They included breathing treatments four times a day and a new chest treatment three times a day, plus trying to get Tom to take in some nutrition without compromising his ability to breathe. He was on the BiPAP machine most of the time and relied on that for his breathing. I could see in his eyes that his light was going out with the exasperation of it all.

I knew I was losing the battle for him. I felt defeated, and I'm sure he was ready to give up the battle, too. But how could I even think about letting that happen? How could I declare defeat for him? When was enough, enough?

I was very sad but tried to keep my attitude positive for

him. I would sing him songs and tell him everything going on outside our home to keep him informed. He had always loved to hear the tidbits of life, even if he could not participate in it.

But now, something had changed. I don't know if it was my dad's passing, or how Tom's disease had progressed. I know now that he sensed his end was near. I, on the other hand, had no clue. I still had those rose-colored glasses on. It had only been two days after Dad's funeral, but it seemed like forever.

That night he aspirated again. I had never seen him like this before and was not sure I was capable of helping him. I asked if he wanted to go to the hospital. He wanted to stick it out and wait until the morning to see if he could work it out and be okay. That night I slept on the floor next to him, with the bell rigged to wake me if he needed me. I tried to stay awake, but eventually did fall asleep.

He did need me. He rang the bell to wake me to help him sit up and try to get the phlegm out. We did a eucalyptus treatment that had always helped in the past. I would put a few drops of eucalyptus oil in a pot of hot steaming water. He would breathe in the fumes with a towel over his head. This had the amazing result of causing the phlegm to come up where he could spit it out—a simple, organic way of helping. It did help this night, although I could tell he was exhausted. His breathing had deteriorated significantly. I thought we should go to the hospital. He declined again.

He was able to get back to sleep and I was able to stay awake on watch for the rest of the night. When morning came, it was apparent that he was not good. His breathing was compromised even though he was on the BiPAP. He could not come off it to drink, eat or do anything. He could not breathe on his own. It was time to go to the hospital. I could not let him die here under my watch. I needed help. He finally agreed.

I called the local ambulance and they came. I had never done this before and did not know what to expect. They came quickly and were very considerate and concerned. They wanted a history and started to strap him into a device to carry him to the ambulance. They strapped him too tight, and Tom could not breathe. He panicked and was distressed. I stopped everything to calm him down and explain that he needed to be on his BiPAP and could not breathe without it. They understood and arranged for power to transport. Perfect. Tom was calm again, but anxious.

We arrived at the hospital and received number one priority. The doctors and nurses descended on us with questions for me and put all kinds of medical apparatuses on Tom. It was a swarm of bees surrounding and poking to quickly learn whatever they could to decide what to do. They did their testing while I recited the memorized sequence of events to the doctors.

Everything was somewhat calm until they obtained a reading that he was having a heart attack!

They said they needed to rush him to cardiac surgery and needed my permission. Yes! There was no thought about this. Save my man! In hindsight, I wonder if that was the right decision, but I was not ready to let him go, nor do I think he would want me to.

We were taken to the cardiac floor, where I signed papers to do an exploratory procedure to determine if there was a blockage to his heart. My brain spun so fast it was impossible to have a single sane thought. He could die on the table, but we needed to do this. I went into the operating room with him and gave him a hug, kiss and told him I loved him, and that he would be fine and I would be waiting for him.

When I walked out of the operating room, my daughter stood there. Oh, my goodness. She was still here in town from my dad's passing and I had texted her what was happening. She found me on the cardiac floor. Incredible! Crazy! Insane! How, who, what put her here through this gigantic maze of a hospital in this space, at this moment, when I needed her most?

We hugged and cried in each other's arms. I explained everything, and we sat and waited for the news, hoping for the best. She told me later that when she arrived there on that floor, she had a glimpse of Tom on the operating table and me crying by his side. She thought he had just died.

The doctor came out with good news. "All arteries are clear!"

"Wonderful! Now what?"

Tom was admitted to The ICU for observation. We were told the next day that he had Pericarditis, which is inflammation of the heart sac. This was in combination with pneumonitis, inflammation of the lungs. Strong antibiotics were prescribed. We stayed in ICU and I slept in the room with Tom.

I went home after two days to take a shower and change clothes but spent all the rest of the time with Tom. He was stable but still struggling with his breathing. The hospital wanted to put him on their "monster" Bipab, because it was their equipment and they could regulate it and monitor it on the screen.

At first Tom objected, but then he decided to give it a try. It was not a positive event. I almost lost him. This machine was very aggressive compared to his. He panicked and could not breathe. Alarms started going off and everyone came to help.

I started talking to Tom loud and clear. "Tom, look at me. You can breathe. Just try. Calm down, look at me and breathe. In and out, in and out." My voice became softer and slower, in tandem with the breathing that I needed. "Take it slow. In and out. You can breathe. You can stay here with me. Don't go. Stay here with me. You can breathe. In and out, in and out, in and out." Almost a whisper in the stark calmness of the room with six nurses and interns watching, holding their breath.

It worked. He calmed down and breathed for the short amount of time it took them to get everything working again. He was alive for now.

One of the nurses took me aside afterwards and asked me if I knew that I just saved his life. I wondered why I tried to save him then and why I did not let him go. It was simple. That was a terrible and terrifying situation for him. I did not want him to die like that. He deserved better. That was my rationale then, but now as I think about it I wonder who I was trying to save, him or me.

Every day was all about trying to get Tom back to normal. Everyone worked toward that end. He was still on the BiPAP one hundred percent of the time. The meds needed to eliminate the inflammation. The doctors came every morning but offered fewer options as the days passed. They recommended he go on a ventilator. Tom did not want that; neither did I. It would prolong the inevitable and make him more miserable than he was now. He had been through hell and back already.

The nurses created a word board for Tom to communicate, since he could no longer use his phone or stylus to text to talk. It was too much effort. He used the board to point to letters, one at a time, to form words.

I had been in touch with his family, sending daily texts of his status. They asked if they should come. Was it the end of this horrible journey? I could not say yes or no. I still had those rose-colored glasses on. They made the decision to come. Thank God! His brother, Chris, his sister, Jenny, and his son, Bryan, came from Florida, which was wonderful for me and for Tom. He was so happy to see them and to spend time with them.

It was especially endearing to see Tom's son with him. He called him "Pops" and brought that twinkle back in his eye. They "talked" football that they both loved and just enjoyed each other's company. They had not had the best of relationships, but this gave Tom the best present he could have received. It was heartwarming to watch them together. Beatles music, all 624 songs played in the background, like we might be enjoying a beautiful concert at strawberry fields forever.

When Jenny and Chris, Tom's sister and brother, arrived, they expanded the board with full words and phrases, especially ones Tom would say. I was so grateful they were here, and that Tom had this special time with them.

We did have others come to visit, but I was content to be in our little world together, with just us. I think I knew, without fully accepting it, that our days together were numbered.

One night in the middle of the night, Tom started fighting something or someone in his sleep. He punched the air and became very upset. He started to pull his mask off. I tried to stop him, and he punched me in the face. I could not believe his strength. I started screaming for someone to help me.

A nurse came in, tried to settle him down and he punched her. She pulled out these big mitts and tried to put them on him. He did not like that at all and started punching madly. It was crazy. I talked to him in a soft voice, telling him that I was here with him and that everything was okay, that he was okay. I told him I loved him and wanted him to stop fighting and be with me. I kept talking to him softly, soothingly. He calmed down while the nurse added a med in IV to help him, too. Finally, he fell asleep.

A doctor showed up and described the occurrence as ICU Paranoia. He said it was common when you were in ICU for a prolonged period without sunlight. It gave you a feeling of not being part of a world and being paranoid.

I asked the nurse if she could get me an extra-large cup of coffee, black, so I could stay up for the rest of the night. I was afraid I would fall asleep and this would happen again. (It never happened again.) Even though he seemed to be sleeping, I talked to him for the rest of the night about our travels together, with all the details I could remember.

After six days, we were moved to the Step-Down floor. This meant you were very ill, but not in intensive care. The inflammations were waning but were being taken over by pneumonitis. Fevers started every day, which required a newer, more intensive antibiotic. Tom's spirits ebbed.

I was still sleeping there and going home to take a shower and change clothes. I had unplugged from everything and everyone, except Tom.

I asked if we could contact our Dr. J, Tom's last doctor who had helped him significantly in the past, to request a mega steroid treatment, to see if this would help like it had in the past. They agreed and started the treatment. It was a five-day process. The result of this mega treatment was that he could not go more than five minutes breathing on his own without the BiPAP. It was not good. We did not have many more options that were acceptable, except for a miracle.

And then it was Mother's Day. I knew my mom was hurting badly from my dad's passing and though I was in desperate times, I decided I needed to go see her. Bryan agreed to sit with Tom while I went to see my mom.

On that drive to Mom's, I put the top down on my car. As the breeze cleared my head, I could finally think clearly. We had to stop the fight. I had to let go and allow him peace. We had to accept the inevitable that this was the end. Tom should not suffer any longer. That is what I had promised him. There was nothing else to do but go home and make him as comfortable as he could be.

I had a visit with Mom and drove back to the hospital with a renewed spirit and objective.

I presented my case to Tom. I told him my opinion. "You have suffered enough and there is nothing the medical community can do for you now. We have done everything and anything we could to help you, but now there is nothing to do but go home and to make you as comfortable as possible. Do you want to continue the fight, or call it?"

He responded with his palms flat, touching each other, then spread out to the sides in the classic sports' hand signal. Call it.

It was what I should have expected . . . he was just waiting for me to accept this. I informed the nurse of our decision and that we wanted to go home tomorrow. I also told her to remove the alarms from the bed, since I would be sleeping with Tom in his bed tonight.

It was so beautiful to be in bed with my love, holding him and whispering sweet love in his ears. He was so fragile I was afraid I might break a bone, but he did not want me to leave him. I told him how he was my knight in shining armor, being so strong and courageous through this fight, and now it was time to stop fighting and just be the beautiful person that he always was. I loved him and would never ever stop loving him. He would always be with me, no matter what.

After he fell into a deep sleep, I got up and spent the rest of the night researching Hospice and the process of dying. I learned what steps needed to be taken to allow a person to die. The nutrition he received via IV had to stop, as well as the meds he was on. He would stay on BiPAP, because he needed it to breathe. He would receive meds at home to allow his body to go through the process of shutting down, make him comfortable, and remove any anxiety he might feel.

I explained all of this to Tom in the morning and asked him if he still wanted to go through with it. He could extend his life further by going on a ventilator. He was firm in his response. He did not want to go on a ventilator. "I understand, and I want to go home now."

The exit manager came to see us, and we explained our wishes. She said that it was not easy to go home on such short notice since so many things had to be in place and decisions had to be made.

Since I had done my research and Tom had made his final decisions, it was easy to finalize everything. The exit manager was wonderful. She was very compassionate and said she would do everything in her power to move us as quickly as possible.

We had a final meeting at the hospital early the next day with Hospice, the doctors, nurses and hospital exit staff. They asked if I wanted the meeting down the hall. I said that Tom needed to be part of it since this was his decision. We would meet in his room.

I did most of the talking, explaining our wishes of stopping all treatment and nutrition and going home with Hospice to help us. I thanked them for everything they had done for Tom and me. It was bittersweet.

After the meeting, in the hall, I asked the Hospice manager if she had any idea how long it would take. She estimated two weeks.

Chapter Twenty-Six
The End

Thank you, my love.

OUR BEST FRIENDS, SUSAN AND DOUG, CAME TO our house while we were still in the hospital and with the help of Steve, one of our wonderful next-door neighbors, rearranged furniture to create room for a makeshift hospital ward. They stayed over and accepted the medical equipment we would need first thing in the morning.

Meanwhile, at the hospital, they had disconnected all treatment, paperwork was signed, and we waited for transport. It was almost like going on a trip somewhere, but this trip was different.

When we got home, everything was set up and ready for Tom. He was so happy to be home. We got him settled in the hospital bed and allowed him to recuperate from the ambulance ride. Then he wanted to sit in his beloved recliner and have that TV remote in his hand again. It was hard for him to work it, but he was diligent and successful to put his favorite sports channel on. He had a big crooked smile on his face and a twinkle in his eyes.

He could sit in his chair only the first two days. After that, he was too weak to sit up. In those first two days, our friends and family came to see Tom and say their goodbyes. Susan and Doug were there to help every moment. They were the greeters, the host and hostess to our company, and my backbone.

At one point, Susan let someone in, and a big orange cat tried to get in the house. Susan, a cat lover, shooed the cat away, commenting that it was odd a cat we had never seen before would try to get into the house. It reminded her of that story about a nursing home where a cat would sit at the door or bed of the next person to die. Then she felt bad that she had said anything about dying. I didn't think anything of it; I had enough on my mind.

I will never forget when my son, Bill, my daughter-in-law, Tara, and my three-year-old granddaughter, JoJo, came. JoJo is my namesake, named Josephine Marie, who is a beacon of happiness. I asked Bill to help me give Tom a boost in the bed and JoJo asked if she could help. She called him Tom-Tom and had been afraid of Tom-Tom in the last few months when they came to visit. We think it was because Tom had changed a lot due to his illness and she did not really understand who he was.

She went up and helped pull the sheet up and kissed his hand. It was beautiful. Tom knew how special this was for her and for him. It was truly a gift that his little granddaughter would not be afraid and could show her love for her Tom-Tom in his last hours.

Then, I had to get down to the business of dying. It was a learning experience for me to understand what options were available to help Tom through Hospice in his final days. The Hospice folks who came to meet with us were wonderful. They were concerned, caring individuals that only wanted to help in the best way possible. They helped me to understand the services available for his care and comfort, as well as what would happen in the final stages of his life. The paperwork was overwhelming, but they cut though it with clear and simplified language that allowed me to quickly make decisions on Tom's care.

They did offer volunteers to come and help bathe, massage or offer religious support, and there was also a listing of private duty nurses who could care for Tom and administer the drugs to keep him comfortable. Tom was not a religious person, and although he was gregarious in his life, this was a very private time for him. I respected his wishes, which made the choice very clear. This was the time that required only me to comfort and nurse him.

My wish came true, to be with him in the end. The windows were open, so he could feel the breeze on his face and smell the fresh May air. The birds were especially delightful in their song on these beautiful May days. I know this was just for Tom. I had his favorite Beatles' songs playing in the background, just like we had done in the hospital. It was soothing and calm.

The cat did not leave. It sat patiently on the lawn facing the kitchen window, looking straight through to where Tom was.

I tried to be in bed with him the first two nights, but he did not seem comfortable, and his comfort was my primary objective. So, I stayed on the couch right next to him, dozing on and off. I don't think I slept much in those last days. My mind was blank, and I was numb, even though outwardly I functioned normally. I hoped and prayed that I was doing everything right.

Tom was still on the BiPAP twenty-four seven. He could not do the letter board any more, but he was comfortable and had a peaceful glow in his eyes. Words were not necessary.

I'm not sure what I thought at this time, except that I wanted him to be as comfortable as possible. I put my emotions on hold and tried as hard as I could to be strong, just like Tom. The idea that his death was imminent did not play any role whatsoever. It was as if it would or could never happen, even though he was fading on me every single moment that went by.

The most important thing I learned from Hospice was to give permission to your loved one to leave. Most people do not want to leave this earth. They feel tied to their loved ones and do not want to leave them. It made all the sense in the world to me that I needed to give Tom permission to leave this earth and die. I had not accepted for the three years prior to this day that Tom would die from ALS, but I did finally accept it.

Susan and Doug stayed and were my anchors. Tom's Aunt Wendy came and gave him the healing touch treatment she had given him in the hospital. I could almost see a glow of energy surrounding Tom while Aunt Wendy went about her healing process.

Dwindling life continued around the clock, with ongoing meds, and me staying by his side. I reminded him of all our good times together and how much fun we had. I talked to him about our wonderful life together and how I would savor every shred of it. No regrets.

The cat stayed poised for whatever his mission was.

The fever started on the fourth day, as they had told us it would. It was ice packs, meds, several changes of clothing, bathing and bed linen changes. The fever finally broke after a full day and night. All that was left to do was to comfort and love him, staying by his side and watching for anything and everything that could happen.

That afternoon and evening there was a big windstorm outside. The breeze came in to help Tom cool down. I told him it was the angels here to take him to a better place. I told him it was okay to go with them. They would take care of him and he would always be in my heart and by my side. It was what he should do.

Hospice told me that our loved ones can hear us even in a coma state, which is the last stage. Tom was in that coma state after his fever broke on the fifth day of being home. I took his Claddagh wedding ring off his finger and told him I would wear his ring proudly forever, and that now he could leave me in body, but never in spirit.

He seemed to be somewhat stable with a strong heart-beat. Even though he was still on the BiPAP, he did not appear to be with us. But I knew he was. I could feel his presence and his love. It was hard to know what would happen next. That diligent cat should have been my cue.

Susan and Doug needed to leave for a short bit while Aunt Wendy was there. They would have stayed if they knew how imminent his departure was.

Wendy and I were on our own and did not know what to expect. We both talked to him, telling him family stories, knowing he could hear us. Wendy decided that she, too, would leave and come back later. Tom looked like he would be fine for a while. She went over to tell him she was leaving, and he let out a gasp of sorts with his head off the pillow. Wendy shouted that she thought he just passed.

I rushed over to his side and checked his pulse and heartbeat. It was very faint. We both tried several times and could not discern if he was still with us or not. The BiPAP was still going, but that was just a machine. We decided not to remove the BiPAP, but it seemed like he had left us.

It felt like he was gone. The air felt differently. We both felt that his spirit had left his body, even though he appeared to be still breathing because of the BiPAP.

We kept checking his pulse and heartbeat for the next twenty minutes, not really knowing if he had passed, but feeling like he had. We commented that we could do a good *Saturday Night Live* routine, asking who can feel a pulse or if a heart is still beating. It was not a reality yet. How do you know?

Death is supposed to be so final, but it really isn't. It can be a state of mind, a machine being unplugged, or a life leaving this earth on the sweet wings of angels. I chose the latter for Tom.

I decided to call the Hospice nurse and ask her opinion. She was five miles away and would be there shortly. She arrived and quickly announced that Tom had indeed passed. She also told us that your own pulse can be felt when you are checking someone else's pulse or heartbeat when it is not there.

Who knew? (As Tom would say.)

I know that Tom gave this last romantic sentiment of au revoir to me. He did not want me to be alone when he died, so he gave it up when Wendy told him she was leaving. He did not have the ability to do anything on his own, but he found a way with his last breath to protect me the only way he could.

Thank you, my Love.

AT–AFTER TOM

"TK"
Thomas Kevin Killmurray

January 31, 1959
May 17, 2014
In Loving Memory

"TK" Coffee
1 Shot Irish Whiskey
1 Shot Irish Cream
8 oz Fresh Coffee
Whipped Cream
Fresh Ground Nutmeg
Cherry For Top

Typically served in a clear mug, ingredients are assembled in the order listed.
Tom would sub any liquor for Irish Whiskey to make a "house" coffee. TK Coffee was named after Tom in Greenwoods Restaurant and served proudly at the Opera Café.

"Sláinte"

(slan-cha) is a word literally translating as "health" and commonly used as a drinking toast in Ireland.

Chapter Twenty-Seven
The Blur

"There is no one who compares to you."

MY LIFE TURNED INTO A BLUR. MY VIEW WAS hampered with rivers of tears, overwhelming heartache and despair, mixed with loving comfort from friends and family. It was a cocktail that I had a hard time swallowing. The only thought that helped was that Tom would remain with me always.

Thank God Wendy was there to help with the final decisions. The funeral home folks came immediately and were kind, helpful and efficient. It was hard to let them take Tom, but I knew it was only his shell. His spirit was still with me in my heart and soul.

The last time I changed and bathed him, I dressed him in my favorite V-neck lavender T-shirt and black and lavender plaid PJ bottoms. I loved how he looked in these clothes, even though they were his sick clothes. It was like I was getting him ready for something special. I wrapped him in his mom's blanket that he loved. His request was to be cremated. He would go in style.

The cat was gone, never to be seen again. Mission accomplished. Unbelievable.

I'm not sure what happened next, except that I remember finally being able to cry. I have not stopped crying, and I'm glad I am able to cry. It helped relieve the pressure and pain inside. It allowed me to extricate every ounce of hurt and sadness that had formed statues in every crevice of my being. I guarded them inside myself because of my love for Tom, so they would never show. I could not let anything negative out and had to be strong and positive every single day of his illness.

Now, I didn't have to do that. I could let years of anguish out through tears, crying, screaming. In the past when I tried to remove this angst through tears, it always came back.

There were still things to do, people to talk to, and the new challenge of figuring out how to deal with all of this. I have no idea how I accomplished anything coherent, but I think and hope that I did not embarrass myself in the process. I really didn't want to see anyone, talk to anyone or do anything with anyone, except my Tom.

That was the only thing I could not do anymore, ever. I could never be with Tom again. He was gone, and I was not. I could not imagine my life without him. I needed him with me always.

The Hospice nurse continued with her duties: finalizing the paperwork and organizing the meds to be destroyed while offering me sage words of comfort. I didn't want to see the meds go; they were Tom's lifeline.

Wendy and I made calls to family and friends. Susan and Doug had just arrived at their home and were freshening up before returning to our home and to Tom. They could not believe that he had passed in their short absence. He saved them from the end, too.

After Tom was taken to the funeral home, everyone wanted to remove all reminders of his death. The kitchen counter was full of meds, special nutrition and assorted Hospice supplies. Everyone helped eliminate the pain; it was dumped into the garbage, where pain belongs. The living room and dining room were full of medical equipment and machines.

"Jo Ann, where can we put all this equipment?"

"I have no idea. Just put whatever you want downstairs anywhere. Just move it out of my sight, please."

"Jo Ann, what should we do with this?"

"I don't care."

Someday in the future, I could give it back or donate it to someone who needed it. But now, I needed to not see it. It was amazing how much stuff we had accumulated to help Tom and to try to keep him alive.

Everyone worked quickly to clear the decks in very short order, except for the hospital bed. The hospital bed reminded me so much of Tom and our love until the end, and how peaceful he was in these last five days. I didn't want to leave it. As I sat there by myself, looking at that hospital bed, the only reminder left of illness, I was finally able to reflect on Tom's passing. The only word that came to mind was *beautiful*. He did not suffer. We were with him through everything until the last second and beyond. His passing was beautiful, serene, peaceful, and what he wanted. We had already suffered the pain of knowing this might be a terminal illness. Now we needed to make it a dream that we could have over and over, feeling like heaven just touched us. I love that dream. Forever.

I'm still not sure how I was able to administer the drugs that would allow his life to end peacefully, and how we both got through it, but I know in my heart that he was as happy as he could be under the circumstances. It was the best ending of an earthly life that could be.

I wonder what happens to one's spirit when they depart this world physically. Some believe the spirit rises to another joyous world without pain and suffering like heaven, never to be heard from again. Others, like myself, believe that a loved one's spirit can stay with us. Is it possible that a little bit of their spirit stays with us and the rest goes to the greater world?

I feel Tom with me and am not sure what that is. Is it my love for him that makes it feel like he is with me? Or is it his love for me that was so strong that it is like a permanent marker, indelible forever? I like to think that Tom's special brand of permanent marker covers me from head to toe. It is an incredible feeling to be bathed in love and know that it will never fade.

Everyone said that I was strong, and if I got through Tom's illness and death, I would be okay. I don't think anyone worried about what I would do, but just wanted to know I was okay. I am an extremely lucky person to have so many incredibly wonderful people in my life. I think I was literally not alone for a long time.

People would call or come over to check in with me. This was a tremendous help and allowed me to operate as a human being every day. I was forced to talk to people and try to be as normal as I could be. The tears were like a spigot that did not have an on or off but ran freely as they wanted. No one cared if I cried, because at least I was feeling and not shutting down.

There were times I just wanted to go into my little lonely nest, turning everything and everyone else off. Then I would dare to reflect on the reality of what happened and think about it all. I couldn't make sense of it, because nothing made sense. But I did feel a dose of relief that I did everything I could have done and that I made him as happy as he possibly could be. I hoped and prayed this was true.

I had this nagging feeling inside somewhere that I was supposed to be doing something, or going somewhere, but I did not know how to do that. It felt as if I was in a glass tube, watching people milling around, near and dear, who tried to help me with food, conversation and pampering; but I was not really functioning, and they could not touch me. I heard everything in muffled tones, as if in the distance where I could not connect with it. I was on autopilot in the fog. That is how I felt, and I wanted that for myself at that point in time. I did not want to go out of the fog in the clear vapor test tube, but death was not an option for me.

I needed to move forward in this new life. Somehow. Some way.

I realize now that I was drifting in a state of life, death, and desolation of grief. I did not wear makeup, had no idea how I got dressed for the day, or if I just stayed in my jammies. People would come and go, checking on me, bringing me food, talking to me. I don't remember who came, what we talked about or even if I ate. I do remember being told that I was functioning better than anyone would have expected. It felt like a mummy experience. Maybe that is how the simplicity all evolved? A mummy wrapped in white to blend into the background and just disappear into space. Pure nothingness felt right.

The next two weeks became even blurrier, like a pelting rain beating down on the windshield of the car so hard that the windshield wipers can't eke out a view in between the raindrops. Tom was gone, and I had to figure out how to live on my own.

And then there were three.

My nephew, Michael J, passed away in his sleep two weeks after Tom passed. It was impossible! He was only forty years old. I was there when he was born. He was too young. Nothing in this life is fair. How much more can we take?

He lived in Florida, close to where my brother, who is in a nursing home and my niece, his sister, live. I received a phone call from my sister, then saw it on Facebook. Shock is the only word to describe the numb feeling that spread through me. He had just posted all his fun escapades the prior day with his friends, doing the things he loved to do.

Michael J was a teddy bear with a style all his own who won the hearts of anyone he met. He was a big guy who could look scary as a bouncer, ready to take you out, but would charm you with his warmth and love. He was like a chameleon since he could change his colors every twenty seconds and look in two directions at once. The chameleon is one of the coolest reptiles on the planet, just like Michael J, but his nickname was Turtle. Not sure how that came about, but he was definitely a turtle, a chameleon and my favorite nephew.

Michael J was a proverbial Miami Dolphins fan, just like Tom, and I was always a New England Patriots fan; the competition was fierce, which kept us tuned into every game together during football season. He was born on my birthday, a very special gift that we shared every year. Otherwise, we loved each other from the distance between Connecticut and Florida. The autopsy report declared that a heart attack snuck up on him that fateful night and took him away from us. I was thankful that we had him for those forty years, but he would be missed every single day.

The blur continued with tears and hurt that felt like it would never leave.

When will it stop?

I had to snap out of it. My family needed me.

The trip to Florida with my mom and sister Deb was painful to say goodbye to another loved one yet satisfying in many ways. Staying with our Florida family helped to pull us together in our grief, knowing we were all feeling pain in different ways for different reasons. We were there for each other. My niece, Danielle, Michael's sister, was in a state of shock, operating on autopilot to make all the funeral plans and host us. There is something to be said for sharing the same pain of loss with more than one person. It helped to know we were not alone.

Then I had to go home to nothing, or so I thought.

Instead I received lots of invitations for dinner, lunch, parties, concerts. I decided that I should partake in life, to try to live the life that Tom would want for me. Participating in life was the one big thing that helped me to survive. It helped to be with people who cared about me, and to have to laugh at something funny. It helped to be forced to function, and to care about what I looked like when I went outside of my home. It helped to take one step at a time, and one day at a time. It is very cliché, but it is true that it is much easier to not have to think about the future. It was hard enough to get through one day at a time without my love, Tom.

I wondered how other people in similar situations as mine got through it all. How did people continue with the world crashing in on you and feeling like an abyss? I realized that people did overcome the worst possible things in their life, and I could, too.

If I didn't have this network of strength, I'm not sure how I would have dealt with it. I think when you are at a precipice in your life, you can jump off the edge, hide under the covers or stand strong. I think I did all of that, and more. I do know that I came through the blur with a mission in mind. I needed to carry out Tom's wishes. That was my mission.

My daughter arrived from Michigan to help me in my endeavor and to keep an eye on my sanity. She is an incredible organizer and doer (just like her mom). She came in and took charge of getting done whatever I wanted. She is amazing! There were so many decisions to make, but it all became very clear and simple how to celebrate Tom's life. It would be at La Zingara's, our favorite restaurant and where we had our first date. The music would be The Beatles and TK coffees would be served. Jennifer designed a card to pass out with a picture of Tom, one of my paintings and the recipe for TK Coffee. Not your typical Mass card, but perfect Tom style.

Tom's brother and sister came up from Florida and the word was passed to family and friends. On the day of the celebration, I was nervous. I wanted this to be special for Tom and was worried about the little details. I wore a beige dress with a kaleidoscope necklace of colorful crystals that Tom would have picked out for me.

I had written a speech and wanted to review it before everyone arrived. I sat at the bar and started making edits and writing notes until the ink ran out of the pen.

Why is this happening? Okay, Tom, enough is enough?

Yes, I had said it all and there was no more to say, according to Tom. This was my first message from Tom.

The celebration was perfect. The people who knew him and loved him came from near and far to talk about the Tom they knew and to share stories. There are a lot of great stories from Tom's many phases of life. It was truly a celebration, a party for a man everyone loved, would miss, and would never forget.

My speech was long and teary-eyed, but the essence of it was true and passionate. I thanked La Zingara for hosting us and thanked our friends and family in attendance. I recounted how we met and how much I loved him.

But the message I delivered that day still rings clear: "Tom was dealt a tough deck of cards, but he handled it extremely well, keeping a positive attitude, being courageous, setting an example and always, always seeing the best in everything and everyone he touched . . . always.

"He ultimately won the game. He is now healthy and whole, watching over me and being with our lost loved ones doing fun things together. As most of you know, my family has had three losses in the past five weeks; my dad Louis, Tom, and my nephew Michael J. It is hard to make sense of it all, but I want to share my thoughts with all of you. Everyone has a certain amount of time on this earth, and we should all make the most of it every day. You could be gone tomorrow. Love the people you love, tell them you love them. Enjoy what you have and savor it. Be positive. It does not help to be negative. Do these things and you will have no regrets. Someone said, God needed a good chef in heaven . . . He got the best . . . Chef Tom.

"Thanks to everyone for the tremendous outpouring of love and support to me and my family during this time and being here today to celebrate Tom . . . love to all of you."

People commented that this was what they wanted when they passed away, a party to celebrate a wonderful life. I don't think a tear was shed until I gave my speech.

I cried, and everyone in the house cried with tears of joy for the love we shared and the special time we all had with Tom.

The finale was an acoustic guitar solo from our good friend Richard. I had called him to request his amazing

216   *Jo Ann Simon*

music, and we said at the same time that the song would and should be "In My Life" by John Lennon. This was Tom's request to me, and this was also what Richard thought was appropriate for us.

I knew the song but had not really listened to the lyrics. When I heard Richard singing those words, I melted on the spot. This was Tom's final tribute and honor to me. You can't imagine how I felt, sitting there with rooms full of the people who knew Tom through family, friends, work, restaurant, school and beyond, but I was the one who stood on that pedestal with this song dedicated to me. It was as if he was talking to all of us. He was remembering everyone in his life and how much he loved and cared for them, and then he shared with everyone that he loved me more.

It was another beautiful moment for me and my love, Tom. He loved me more.

Chapter Twenty-Eight

The Found Recording

I settled into the couch with . . . a box of tissues . . .

BY ACCIDENT, I FOUND A VOICE RECORDING OF Tom and me. It was a piece of us that was buried in the deep dark recesses of life.

It was in June, three weeks after Tom had died. My daughter, Jennifer, her husband, Greg, and my two grandchildren, Esther and Elijah, had stayed since my father died, and for Tom's Celebration of Life. Their presence was a breath of fresh air.

My good friends, Karolyn and Dick, hosted a dinner for us which happened to be on the same day as the Belmont Stakes.

Watching the Stakes and enjoying the procession of horses reminded me of Tom's grandmother Mimi who was a horsewoman in her day.

My granddaughter Esther was fascinated with the horses and stayed glued to the screen. I promised to play the recording of Mimi's poem that she wrote about her horse, Tom, before bedtime that night. Esther thought it was really special to have a horse named after her Tom-Tom.

218 Jo Ann Simon

"Grammy, I would love to hear that poem." Even at seven years old, she was enamored with the arts.

"Esther, we recorded Mimi reciting her poem. I will play it for you when we get home."

"Thanks, Grammy."

It was very late when we arrived home, but Esther would not go to bed without hearing that recording. So, I found the tape recorder, and we all sat in a circle to hear it. I turned it on and Tom's voice filled our space. He was with us.

I faintly remembered Tom recording us one night just before midnight, years ago. I could not believe my ears!

I stopped the recording and found Mimi's poem, which Esther loved, then off to bed she went. I could not think of anything but hearing Tom's voice again and knowing what was recorded.

With Esther tucked in and everyone else off to bed, I settled into the couch with a pillow, blanket, box of tissues, ear phones and a magical recording.

The recording is a tapestry of us the way we always were —a typical couple in love, with the laughing, crying, fighting, making up, making love, as they do. It all happened with beautiful, classic forties music playing in the background. Memories that you can hear and almost touch. A treasure.

When I first listened, I was shaken to the bone just hearing his deep, throaty voice. It was if he was in the room talking to me. I thought it would be a short snippet, but it kept going for an hour and ten minutes. I stayed up until dawn, listening to it four more times until I eventually cried myself to sleep. But in my dreams, I was sitting in the theatre watching this scene on the big screen, in that motion picture of our life.

It captured a critical time in our lives, when our relationship was as precarious as two moths flitting about a light, trying to decide what they want in life. When I listened to this amazing piece of history, I was sobered to hear how beautiful our love was from afar. I could feel through his words, kisses, and touch how much Tom loved me and how carefree he could be.

It also showcased what a bitch I was, and that "we" as a couple were in danger of losing each other for reasons we did not realize at the time.

The first words on the recording are Tom's: "Ray Anthony with Dick Noel doing "A Dreamer's Holiday"—Jo Ann and I at home right before midnight. Let's see what happens."

Climb aboard a butterfly an' take off on the breeze. This is where Tom lived his life: on the back of a butterfly. Even after his illness, he was a dreamer who in some ways didn't care about the reality of the world around him. He was on holiday from reality in his mind, living life *à* la mode, expecting the best from everything.

So, on that night, four years ago before he started to become ill, he was truly on top of the world on a dreamer's endless holiday.

Unfortunately, I was not on that holiday. I lived only in reality and, on that night, was trying to work through resentment, anger, and exhaustion from working full-time and shouldering the debt from the closing restaurant, while trying to make ends meet. He was on permanent unemployed holiday, ignoring responsibility. And yet, he had the innate ability to bring me along with him some of the time. He made me feel like I was the only person in the world who counted and that he would do anything in the world to make me happy. His world was one in which anything terrible could be transformed into something wonderful.

This was where Tom lived his life, on the back of a butterfly. He was always on a holiday from reality in his mind. Life was good, fun and a constant adventure.

The recording went on, with us talking about that night.

Tom: "Wasn't it a wonderful night?"

I did not agree. "Well, it turned into a nice night at the end, but when I got there it was a disaster."

"What do you mean?"

"Tom, you were incoherent."

"In what way was I incoherent?" he asked with a flourish of disagreement.

"You were drunk, and I asked you the same question three times and you could not answer it. You were on a mission."

He tried to defend himself: "But I stopped drinking and then I became coherent?"

"Yes, you did, Tom, afterwards."

He was warming up. "And didn't we have a wonderful dance?"

"Yes, we did."

Encouraged, Tom continued: "Didn't you love that?"

"Yes, I did."

This was not enough. I could not help myself, asking, "I need to know, are you seeing someone else?"

He was surprised and offended. "I am not seeing anyone else and will never see anyone else. I love you and only you. You know that I enjoy the girls and they enjoy me, but you are the only one for me. Why would you ask that?"

It took me a long time to form the words that were hard to say. "We don't make love anymore, you don't bring me flowers anymore. It seems like you don't love me anymore, so the only conclusion is that there is someone else."

He was shocked. "Honey, there is no one but you. I don't know why we don't make love now. You know that my testosterone is low, which is part of the problem, but I just don't feel amorous and don't know why. It's not you. It is me. I don't know what it is, but my body feels differently; something is changing. I have not bought you flowers because I'm not working, and I don't have funds to buy your flowers, even though I want to. It doesn't mean I don't love you."

I felt some relief. He was my man, and he loved me as I loved him. We would work through this together.

Tom knew when a change of subject was needed. He talked about the music in the background and how this was Mimi's era and how grand she was in her day. He said that he should have been born at this time, since he would fit right in, but then he might not have met me.

Throughout all this there was clinking of glasses and sounds of kissing and hugging each other. There had been a lot to drink that evening before we came home, and it did not stop, which is why all our deepest thoughts and fears came out.

If he had not been amorous in the past year, he certainly was that night. He made love to me in the most beautiful and tender way. He spoke to me in a way that made me his.

"You are my gardenia. You are colorful, resilient and beautiful and I will love you always."

Even though this man did everything possible to make me happy, the resentment of thinking he was cheating on me still lingered. His words and love that night did soften me to the point that I could love him and want him forever.

Then the fighting started. We were talking about nonsense, but it did not matter because we would not remember it in the morning. He pointed out that he could play it back!

I said, "Play it back, I don't care, because I'm right."

As we always did, we agreed to disagree and stopped fighting without playing it back. Tom tried to put it all into perspective. "Someday, we are going to play back this tape recording, and we will have fried chicken and cold beer, listening to it. It will be wonderful."

It was always about the food.

Last words on the tape. Tom: "Communication sign off . . . 12:54 p.m. Unbelievable." Said with utter relief, exasperation, and awe of an incredible experience.

This found recorded treasure was a classic reminder of our life, our love, and how dear we were to each other in our own ways with subtle, telling words of impending doom.

Chapter Twenty-Nine

The Doubt

I would just start crying . . .

HOW TO GO ON AFTER ALL OF THIS? WHAT DO I *do? Who am I and who do I want to be? How do I want the rest of my life to be? I am not alone with all the wonderful family, friends and coworkers that I have, but I'm feeling alone at the end of the day.*

I had been trying to save the world, and now I didn't have a world to save. That world was gone forever. I had been a one-armed paperhanger riding a unicycle, trying to balance everything in my life, job, home, doctors, nurses, medicine, treatments, and anything possible to make Tom comfortable.

Now, I had nothing except a deep, empty hole in my heart, my soul and my world.

I'm the type of person who likes to have constant activity and challenges of any kind, but now I wanted to do nothing and be nobody. I didn't have Tom to boost me up and make me happy with that wonderful, crooked smile of his. The look in his eyes when he looked at me would fill me with love down to my toes. He was my reason for the smile on my face and in my heart. He made me want and need to make our world the best it could be every day.

That was gone now, or so I thought.

I didn't know if I could stay in that other world without Tom. I wanted to just feel sorry for myself and crawl under a warm fuzzy blanket, dreaming of the life Tom and I had before the end. If I stayed in that dreamland, lying down with those firecrackers in my hand and pretending to be grass again, I would not have to participate in the real world. I would not have to communicate with people or smile, decide what to say, or get back to normal, whatever normal was now. I didn't want people to feel awkward meeting me, sharing their condolences, or being uncomfortable if I began to cry.

I did cry a lot at home and in public, but I was never ashamed of it or worried about what people thought. I didn't care. Crying was a rite of passage, and it felt good to cry. It felt like a little bit of the hurt would come out with every tear, or every bucket of tears. I felt so alone, empty of everything and anything alive. The tears proved I was still alive, and they acted as my shield from the world I did not want to return to.

But, those rose-colored glasses sitting on the shelf glared at me and my mental state. I could hear the chant in a soft, delicate, captivating way.

"Be positive, you can do it . . . Tom would want you to live your life in a good and meaningful way."

When I did venture out, I talked a lot about Tom: who he was, how I loved him, how he made me so happy. This made me feel good, and I think it was a way to keep him part of me, of us.

I also talked about how beautifully he died. I only told the last part to the people close to me who wanted to know. I think it made them feel better. Talking about death allowed me to realize the comfort of knowing I did the right thing for him. Maybe most people don't associate the word beautiful with death, but in our case, it reflected our love at the worst possible moment in time.

I was still stuck with doubt about what to do and who or how to be without him. I have a strong personality, but I am a very shy person who was still in shock that Tom was gone. I was numb, with an ache in my core I could not stop, an overwhelming feeling of helplessness and emptiness. I felt empty of spirit and life.

The chant continued: "Be positive that you can do this. You can live your life again."

Nothing was normal anymore. I had to figure out what the "new norm" was going to be. This came down to the everyday routines of when to get up, whether to shower or not, get dressed or not, what to eat or not eat, whether to answer the phone or not, and what to do. It was daunting.

Some days I would just sit and cry, dry my eyes, and then cry again. My mind was a blank, a blessed blank.

One day, I decided that I did have responsibilities and I should go back to work. I had an incredible work team that took care of business during the seven weeks I was gone, and even before that when I worked from home and was not totally available. That organized environment surrounded by supportive coworkers made it so much easier to come back to work.

The chant helped me decide to move forward one day at a time and try to be positive. This was not easy to do, but the challenge helped me to work toward putting those glasses on again.

At first it was hard to get back into the routine and have normal conversations with my customers and coworkers.

I tried to be myself, whatever the hell that was, to make it easier for everyone. I knew I would never be the same person that I was before, but I hoped that the person I would turn into would be a better person. Hope is the glue in the sandwich. It can be mayo, butter or mustard, but it makes the difference of holding yourself together or falling apart.

Most people who knew me would ask if I had started painting again. "No, not yet," was the standard answer. My "Painting A Day" blog was like an abandoned boat in the sea of art. During Tom's illness, my only focus was on how to save his life, there was no time to be creative in my art world. So, I closed the door to painting and posting on my blog. It will still be there for me, when I am ready.

It's interesting to me that I had no real want or need to paint. Most people would think that it would be a great getaway and stress reliever. My mind was still too full of doom and gloom; it could not produce a good painting. I doubted my worth and my talent so completely, that there was nothing inside to put into art.

Trying to paint would conjure up all the deep, dark muck that could never look good on a canvas. I remember viewing the Blue Period of paintings by Picasso and feeling such sorrow and distress from those paintings. I think this inner despair and reluctance translates into the ongoing feeling that I failed Tom in some way because I could not keep him alive and healthy. I know this is a crazy thought. I did what I could do and tried everything in the book plus more, but the doubt lingers in my brain, in my heart and in my person.

Instead of painting, I chose to write, to document everything that happened in our lives, so that I would never ever lose any part of our love and our life together. This idea gave me a glimmer of hope for saving myself from an empty life. It felt like the right thing to do.

Remembering was easier than I thought it would be. The memories flow easily, with time to think about what happened and to analyze it all. It was hard to remember the tough times, and the pain and anguish we both had at different times throughout it all. But the memories are wrapped with care, tied with a double knot bow for safe-keeping. They are a stunning gift of the good and the best times we shared together before and during Tom's illness.

I do know that I will paint again with the confidence I had, and maybe with more confidence for better work. I sincerely hope so. I do look forward to it someday.

So, for now, I step back to self-exploration, to review this new me in my lone state, to assess and decide what's next.

I loved my life with Tom, but my inner voice always questioned my existence in this world, and if I was being a good person, doing the right thing, and making the right decisions. The question I constantly asked myself: "Do I wait to see what life brings me, or do I decide where I want to go with my life?"

Tom understood that question mark inside me. He knew when I was on the fence, tiptoeing my way back and forth trying to decide what to do. Then he'd say the prover-bial words: "Do what you want to do, be who you want to be, and go where you want to go." Always the right words from a favorite song that would make it all clear. My deci-sion became much easier after he spoke those words. Now, he sings these words to me on the radio, always at the right time.

Every day decisions form your future and before you know it, ten years have gone by and you have not accom-plished anything except continuing to live. This is the story of my life.

I'm not complaining. I have had an incredible full life with two marriages, finding the love of my life, having two incredible children that I love intensely and call my friends as well; eight cherished, beautiful grandchildren that make me smile just thinking of them, a great job, a comfortable home with a myriad of family and friends.

But, is that all there is to life? Is that all I want? One side of my brain says YES! My life is full and satisfying. The crazy side says NO, maybe there is more for me around that next corner.

Maybe I should push myself to explore the big world of opportunity out there. Life is like a fat wallet, bulging with opportunity. You have to choose how to spend your life.

I know I will figure out who I am again. I will never be the same person I was before, with Tom, but my goal is to be strong, confident and humble to the world around me. When sunshine points the way, it is easy to close your eyes and ears to everything around you and let it take you where it will.

In my case, I had to turn off the entire world and focus on helping Tom. It was as if I was on a different planet with oxygen to breathe and anything I could want, but I just wanted my Tom—the way he used to be, my wonderful, lovely husband Tom.

That was my dream with my rose-colored glasses on.

But, dreams are for dreamers and then the fog lifts and there is an entire, completely different world around you. The alternative is to come out of the fog into the clear air and see what's on the other side.

I decided I should not keep my eyes and ears closed; I should I take a peek out with those rose-colored glasses on.

Chapter Thirty

The Amazing Spirit

Love you forever . . .

11-17-14

Dear Tom,

    Today marks six months since you departed this world and me. I am sadder than I have been every prior month since then. I don't know why today is any different than all the one-hundred-and-eighty days that have gone by, but I know that I miss you more than I can breathe today. It is hard to still imagine my life without you. I feel your spirit with me, but it is not enough. I want to hold you and kiss you and hear your wonderful hearty laugh. I need to hear you whisper sweet words in my ear. I sit here remembering all the wonderment of our love and our short life together. I still cannot believe that you are actually gone.

Where are you? What does it feel like? I know you are close because you send me songs every day. Today was Ringo Starr and "Photograph." It was a perfect song about looking at your pictures every day and remembering where we went together. We had such good times in our travels far and near. I savor those pictures of you and of us and wish we could do it again and again. But that will not be a reality, just a dream.

I tend to dream more now than I ever did before. I dream of you and us and how I can survive this crushing sadness that envelops me.

I need to breathe.

I HAD THE SORROW AND PRIVILEGE OF EXPERI-
encing death and the afterlife at an early age. I was ten years old when my mom died. My mom and dad were separated, waiting for a divorce. I lived with Mom, and my brother lived with my dad. My mom was my world, my heroine, and my lifeline. She treated me with a soft cozy love that always made me feel like I was the most special person in the whole world. Even at that young age, I learned how to have confidence in myself for who I was and what I wanted to be. She had the utmost confidence in me with anything that I did. I took piano lessons, and she would tell everyone that her Jo Ann was going to play at Carnegie Hall one day.

We were girly girls and loved to dress up and be pretty. She was Irish to the bone, with dark auburn hair and strik-ing brown eyes, porcelain skin laced with lovely freckles and luscious ruby red lips, always. She was tall and shapely, but slim as a model. She was the classiest woman I have ever known.

I received the brown eyes and carefree confidence from her, but my skin is from my dad's Italian heritage. I have olive mellow skin that always tans and doesn't burn, plus the extra pounds that are so Italian.

That night, she was going to New York City to see a show. I did not want her to go and pleaded with her to stay home with me; but plans had been made, and she was going. My mom loved to go out and do things, enjoy life and have fun. She gave me that spark to love life and make the most of what you have.

She calmed me by saying, "Sleep in my bed and when I come home I will cuddle with you in your sleep, and you'll know that I'm here with you. Love you, my darling."

I agreed and kissed her goodnight and wished her a fun night. Her girlfriends stayed at our house, babysitting me, playing cards and probably having a drink or two. They were my safety net, there for me and my mom.

In the middle of the night I woke up to screams and hysterical crying from downstairs. I went to the top of the stairs, frozen with fear. I sat on the top stair in the dark, trying to wake up and figure out what was going on. I heard words that didn't make sense.

"She can't be dead!"

"How could this happen?"

"She's gone!"

"I can't believe Marion is dead!"

The raw emotion that curled up the stairs touched me like nothing I had ever felt before. A monster had entered our house and was coming to get me. My hair stood up straight on my arms, a chill ran through my body. I didn't know what to think or do. I could not imagine tiptoeing down the stairs to find out what happened, because that might make it real.

I couldn't ask the question, "Where is my mom?" I wanted to stay far away from the horrible monster, hysteria, that was downstairs. I just wanted my mom.

I was stuck like glue to that top stair, shivering in the darkness, with a glimmer of light touching the bottom steps. I scrunched myself over to the side, trying to hide and hold onto the railing, just to hold onto something that felt real. I knew I was in my home waiting for my mom to return to me, but I also felt lost in the feeling of loss and death that screamed from downstairs.

I started to cry softly with little rivers of tears from my eyes, feeling loss that I had never known before in my ten years on this earth. Something came over me and swept me into this valley of tears. I was in a place to cry as much as I needed to, even though I did not know why I was crying. It was the monster chasing me and I was scared. I did not feel any strength to fight this monster. I tried to stop crying, but I could not.

Suddenly, I felt a cool, clear breath of something surround me. I was afraid to open my eyes, but I convinced myself that it would feel better than the obtuse, dark universe I was in. I needed a good fairy to cut through the bad monster surrounding me.

I was brave enough to open my eyes, to see my mom in an image, floating on the flat wall in front of me, above the stairs. She was right in front of me, smiling at me.

She said, "Jo Ann, I love you and you need to know I will always be with you. I will sit on your shoulder to guide you and help you when you need me. Tell me if you need me. I know you will be okay because you are smart, brave and strong. You have nothing to fear. I love you always and will be with you."

She said all that needed to be said, and then she was gone. I felt this glorious, wonderful blanket of warm love and peace cut through the monster that lurked with ugliness and darkness. It was then that I thought she might really be gone from this earth.

But she would never be gone from me, and that filled my heart with a warm spot that allowed me to go back to bed as if I knew nothing. She would be with me no matter what happened. I was sure of it.

I fully hoped she would come home that night and wrap her arms around me with cuddles and love, like she said she would. I fell asleep thinking that maybe, just maybe, this other thing was only a dream.

I feel her with me from time to time, even fifty plus years after a cerebral hemorrhage took her from me at the young age of thirty-eight. I hope and pray this will always be true. I don't know how to make that happen except to be open to it and to want the connection. It's not like you can put it into a calendar or set a timer. It is a greater power than anything on this earth. It makes me feel like there are wonderful, surprising and magical things, even if logically they seem impossible. You have to believe this power exists and that these people have the power to touch us if we believe they can.

The connection I have had with my deceased mother since my childhood made it easy to believe that Tom, too, would always share my life in mysterious, touching ways. He could put a smile on my face and give me a way to find my path to live life again without him on this earth.

Small signs helped me. It became clearer every day that I needed to open my eyes and ears to look and listen to the signs that my dear departed loves left for me. These signs gave me the energy I needed to believe that life was still worth living, and that they were still with me in so many ways, as well as in my heart.

As I embraced what I heard and saw, I began to feel a sense of being embraced. I could accept that they were not on this earth anymore, but they walked and talked with me in subtle, beautiful ways.

In the first one hundred days after Tom's passing, amazing things happened that could only be from Tom's spirit. The week after he had died, songs came to me every day, on the car radio or in a restaurant; meaningful songs that were his way of communicating with me. They were unusual songs one normally does not hear on the radio, like "Somewhere over the Rainbow" and "You Are My Special Angel," which was his signature song for me.

The first time I heard "Somewhere over the Rainbow," I was in a nail salon with Susan, getting pedicures together. Previously there was crazy Latin music on the overhead speaker, and then it was quiet for a second. I had been telling Susan about the songs and, when it started playing, she looked at me with her mouth open . . . "Oh my God, it's Tom. Yes, it is."

I have heard more versions of "Somewhere over the Rainbow" than I had ever heard before. Who knew Ella Fitzgerald sang that song? But my favorite is the version by Hawaiian Israel "IZ" Kamakawiwo'ole. Tom plays that when I least expect it, and it feels like he is singing it directly in my ear.

One day, I was driving down the road crying, thinking of Tom and wondering if I should pull over to finish crying and not crash the car. Suddenly, "Sunshine, Lollipops and Rainbows" came on the radio. When I was upset about something, Tom would sing this song to me with his hands waving in the air like a funny clown. It was his cheer-up song just for me. He was trying to tell me to stop crying and everything would be okay, and it worked.

I was in Cleveland visiting Mimi; a promise I kept since she could not come to Tom's Celebration of Life. I went to Sokolowski's in Cleveland to have their world-famous pierogies. Tom always said this is a place you have to go if you are in Cleveland, so I went.

From the outside, it looked like a fancy Tudor house. The inside was a few rooms with dark wood, checkered tablecloths and a festive feel that makes you feel like you are in Europe on holiday. It was unassuming, with a self-serve cafeteria-style food section and a long line of people. Everyone seemed excited to be in that long line. They talked about the food and what to have. They said I had to have the pierogies. Or the walleye fried fish. Or the stuffed cabbage.

Handmade paper signs touted the special of the day: six pierogies and one potato pancake for eight dollars. That sounded perfect to me.

When I had my tray with gorgeous pierogies, I looked for a place to sit. The music from the piano drew me in. I followed the lovely sound and found a big room with a gentleman playing the piano. When I sat down and put the first bite in my mouth, he started playing "Somewhere over the Rainbow." Coincidence? No. How could Tom be with me but not with me? How is this possible? Don't ever let it stop, please.

I went up when I was done and put some cash in his basket and thanked him for the beautiful song. I told him that my husband sent that song for him to play and it was more special than he could imagine.

"Thank you, beautiful one, come back soon," he said.

This was exactly what Tom would say. He would ask me the same question every day. "Did anyone tell you how beautiful you are today?" I would always say no. He would say, "Jo Ann, you are beautiful on the inside and out." I would smile, say, "Thank you, darling," give him a kiss and tell him, "I love you."

One day after he was gone, my phone spoke to me out of the blue. I had downloaded his text-to-talk phrases from his phone to mine, just so I could listen to them and keep them to remember. I was in my car, my phone fell, and suddenly, I heard, "Honey, did anyone tell you how beautiful you are today?" Of course, I had to answer no. There were no further words from Tom, but there was a feeling of being loved.

When I arrived home after my visit to Mimi, life continued without my participation, just like when Mom died.

I had always loved to shop but had not done any shopping except for the essentials for a long, long time. I had company coming and while making up the spare room, I decided I should get some new pillowcases.

I went to the local home goods store and seemed to sleepwalk in circles, looking at everything but seeing nothing. Normally I would have a cart full of finds I could not bear to leave behind. This day, nothing appealed to me. I could not imagine carrying something out of the store and then exerting more energy to do something with it.

I roamed around and around like a zombie, just to be out, instead of home feeling sorry for myself. I found the pillowcases and decided it was time to go. Heading toward the front, a little voice in my head said, "Go down that aisle." I turned and saw a row of throw pillows in every shape, color and size. Halfway down the aisle, I saw it: a rectangular, long pillow, white with aqua trim with script letters in aqua saying:

love you forever

I was elated. I was not alone. Tom was telling me, as he always did, that he loved me forever; but what he also told me was to get out of my doldrums, do something fun!

So, I decided to redecorate my bedroom around that pillow. I was not a zombie anymore, I was on a mission. I spent another hour in the store, filled my cart, and could not wait to get home to change over my bedroom. I felt an energy build in me to do something just for me, something to comfort me and make me feel like I was in a better place.

I could begin my transformation in my own home. That cold, gloomy blanket of grief slowly started to come undone. I wondered why I had not found this positive ray of sunshine on my own. Why did I wallow in my sadness until a sign, a touch, or a message came from Tom? It had felt as if it was midnight with an overcast sky that hid the moon and the stars. Suddenly, a shooting star would light up the sky to show the reflection of light and beauty. You would want to stay up all night in the darkness just to see that light again and what it felt like.

I knew that grief was the culprit, and I was lost in my loss. I needed that shooting star to show me the way to find my path back to reality and to myself.

I was encouraged by this intimate message from Tom. I had been the fighter, the one with the upbeat, we can do anything attitude, but I had lost that with my loss of Tom. He turned into the cheerleader now! He was the one with the positive attitude. I was thankful for this sweet nudge to point me in the right direction. I knew the rest was up to me.

There were many, many songs, and many incidents that told me in special ways that he would always be by my side, watching over me.

When you are so close to someone for so long with a connection that outspeaks volumes of books, it makes sense that we can't just cut the cord one day and no longer be part of them and vice versa. I can't explain it, but I love the feeling of Tom surrounding me and holding me up. It is as if I am floating on water with a special serum in my blood that makes me buoyant. I do feel my dad, my nephew, my mom, but not as strong as I feel Tom.

He showed me by his touches from beyond that I would not lose him if his ashes were cast in the waters of Key West. He would still be with me. That thought gave me the strength and energy to schedule the perfect trip to the Keys.

It was time to honor his wishes at the waters of Key West.

Chapter Thirty-One
Key West Segue

Hog's Breath, of course . . .

A WISH AND A WONDER—THE PERFECT SEGUE from grief.

It had been Tom's specific request. "Jo Ann, I want to be cremated and my ashes to be cast in the waters of Key West behind Hog's Breath Saloon." Where he'd asked to marry me.

The entourage was organized. Tom's siblings and their spouses, Chris, Jessica with their two children, Aubrey and Colin, Jenny and her partner, Nicole. My good friend, Janet, asked to join us—an extra special addition to the group. My niece Danielle, her husband, Danny, and their son, Jayden, would meet us in Key West.

We would start in Tavernier, mile marker 91, at my good friend Gary's house, which sits on the edge of eternity with a view that feels like an unending existence spreading across the infinite aqua waters. Mile markers in the Florida Keys are set relative to the number of miles north of Key West. Tom and I had stayed here a few times, and we adored the comfortable Floridian feel of the house, with the unique view and a family of jade iguanas to entertain us.

Tom's trip did not get off to a good start at Westchester Airport. I had packed his ashes in individual baggies stored snuggly in his favorite wool socks, packed into a tall cardboard bottle holder with a lid. Everything fit perfectly. The print on the bottle holder was covered with corks of different varieties, and several with just a fancy *K*, which was his last name initial. I wrapped the container in festive wrapping paper and tied it with a bow. I purposely had it stowed in my carry-on. I couldn't imagine putting him in my checked suitcase and being separated. I hoped and prayed we would breeze through security.

The Westchester Airport was small, and the security lines were backed up with anxious flyers, trying to be respectful of those in front of them. I was especially anxious with my special parcel.

We, Tom and I, did not make it through without questions. The security officer was an older gentleman with a stern look on his face, very official and formal: "May we search your bag?"

"Yes." The tears started brimming. I didn't want to have to explain.

"What is in the container?" The tears started rolling, first down one cheek, then the other.

I whispered, "My husband's ashes."

Everything and everybody stood still, as if I had shouted this at the top of my lungs.

The officer then became soft and compassionate. "I am very sorry for your loss. Unfortunately, we will need to verify, with full respect for your husband."

We went to a corner by ourselves and I unwrapped and opened the package showing the officer what was inside. Then he helped me put it back together again and sent me on my way. I deeply appreciated the respect of the officers. Only after we reached our gate could I exhale.

I knew I should have handled this by the book and communicated with the airline, but I couldn't bring myself to do it. I felt like this was a private journey and I did not want to share it with strangers. It was bad enough that I couldn't save him. Why would I inform the officials that I could not keep my husband alive?

I survived the airport incident, and the group banded together to squash the solitary sadness that we all felt.

The first night started a new feeling of celebratory melancholy that spread like wildfire amongst us, to curb the tears when they started, or pull out the buckets to contain them when they wouldn't stop. The best part was just being together to share our pain and to bolster each other up with hugs, stories and cocktails, lots of cocktails. This was the crossword puzzle that Tom would have created with the clue: Tight Families.

Toward the end of the first night, I took a picture of everyone on the deck, then Jessica switched to get a picture with me in it. The second picture had a shadow next to Chris, as if someone stood next to him, someone with an undeniably familiar profile. No one else had moved, but it was obvious that Tom was in the picture, too. He was with us. He was happy that we were all together, fulfilling his wish.

Dear Tom,

Do you know that I have this lovely soft spot in my being that comes from you? I love this place in my heart and soul that you created. It has the essence of a sultry sweet hum that fills me with a feeling of arms wrapped around me making me feel loved, precious and content. You have that ability to love me from afar when you were on this earth and your powers of persuasion still work from heaven or that next room that you are in. Don't ever stop. I hope that you feel my love, too, that I send every day. We are one and always will be.

Goodnight, My Love

The next morning, my eyes popped open as if someone had pulled the eyelashes up to see what was inside. It was the weirdest feeling.

I lifted the blind and was greeted with a glint of gold shining on me. I grabbed my phone and tiptoed to the back deck. My first daybreak on the Keys filled me with awe. It was astonishingly beautiful to see the birth of this day in this place.

That's when it hit me—Tom had woken me up! He always stayed up to see the sunrise; I could never make it that far into the night. The sunsets were my cat's meow. He opened my eyes this morning to show me that there is another day, there are many days ahead, and I should be part of them.

Thank you, Tom. The amazing images of that sunrise remind me to live every day.

Our segue continued to Key West. The weather was balmy and our breathtaking drive down Route 1 surrounded us with delicious endless water and wildlife that uplifted our spirits.

Mile Marker 0 was the beginning of the end of Tom's road. But before we arrived at our destination, we retraced our steps to the favorite haunts that we treasured when we had visited many times together.

We loved all the flavors of Key West. La Te Da's was the best breakfast in Key West. My fantasy of Blackstone Benedict came true again. Our stops also included Hog's Breath, of course, with the same margaritas as when he proposed; and the Rum Bar, for the perfect Dark 'n' Stormy that Danny had never had and fell in love with. We all barely fit into The Smallest Bar.

We continued our roaming around, celebrating Tom at every stop, from one end of town to the other, eventually returning to our place and hanging out at the pool with the palms and the balminess of Key West surrounding us.

As we sat there relaxing and soaking up the sun, I asked Tom's brother, Chris, to tell me something about Tom that I didn't know.

"One day when I visited last March, just the two of us sitting on the couch, I asked Tommy if he had any regrets and is there anything he still wanted to do. He said, 'No, Chris, I've had the finest wine, I've eaten the best food in the world and none of that compares to the love of my life. To win the love that we have had in this world is all that I need.'"

This was so beautiful to hear. Chris went on to add one more discussion with Tom. "Tommy always said that he looked up to me, his little brother, for the courage I had for being in the Army and going to war. I told him he was the one with the courage, especially how he faces this disease with grace and dignity, taking it head-on, fighting it like hell. I told him, 'Just so you know, Brother, you will always be my hero in courage for how you handled yourself in life, love and, of course, food. I will carry all those things with me.'"

The love of two brothers is truly something special. I will carry them, too.

The next day brought finality in many ways. Chris and Jenny had organized a captain and boat to take us out to cast Tom's ashes. I would do the Ice Bucket Challenge for ALS. It was fitting and right to do both on the same day. I had wanted to do the Challenge but was still in denial that it was ALS that had taken his life. I knew in my heart that it was, but my brain could not accept it. It still did not make sense to me.

The debate continued. Did I do everything I could? Everything I should have done to save Tom? How did this happen? Should we have lived our lives less gregariously so that he could have lived longer, or would that have caused us to not live life to the fullest, and not be as happy as we were? I say we, but he was ten times more gregarious for ten times longer than me. So, you could do the math and say that his life would absolutely be shorter than mine and it's actually amazing that he lasted this long.

In the relatively short time that I knew Tom, we took advantage of every opportunity to enjoy every day, every moment. We traveled extensively, ate at the best restaurants, owned a restaurant together, worked hard, and played as much as we could fit in. We enjoyed our families and friends by spending time, laughing and crying together.

How we loved each other was the best testament of a good life. We also had our calamities of life as all people do, but if you had to measure the fullness of our lives, we would have measured full to the brim.

Right now, I would measure half-empty with a leak from all my tears.

My theory is that everyone has a number. When your number is up, you are taken from this earth and transported to a place where peace surrounds your heart and soul.

The question remains: Could I have changed destiny? Should you let fate take you down the road to what your real destiny is?

Of course, we have daily decisions that may change our paths, but I believe that fate will follow no matter where you go or try to hide. It has a way of attaching a string to your little pinky, like a comfortable ring you don't ever want to take off. This string allows fate to watch over you and guide you down its path, even if you don't want to go that way. I felt that string tugging me when I was trying desperately to find a way to save Tom.

I will always wonder if I should have found other doctors, other hospitals, or medicine in other countries. I will always wonder if we should have accepted the ALS diagnosis sooner. I think if we did, that tiny string of fate would have strangled us before we were ready to give it up.

So, I will try to live and make the most of each day. I will also try desperately to have no regrets.

ALS is still a horrible disease. So, if I could spread my husband's ashes in Key West with respect and love, I could pour a bucket of ice water over my head for the good of everyone else out there who is suffering with this horrid disease called ALS. I wanted to do my little part to help and pass that on. It was smart of me to do it in the warmth of Key West, to cool me down and blend with my tears.

It is incredible what the Ice Bucket Challenge has done for the people suffering from ALS. Finally, someone did something to help the tiny world of ALS. Someday, there will be a cure just because those funds will allow the researchers to spend the time they need to find that cure. This wonderful marketing strategy is opening the eyes of the world. It will save lives.

Our merry band turned somber as our boat made its way to the chosen spot. The background was perfect, with cream puffs of clouds in the surreal sky giving us their nod for the right location. The sun was busy organizing its daily escape.

The captain stopped, dropped anchor and the quiet chitchat came to an end, while we contained our thoughts and felt the mood.

Light winds caressed us as if to say, "It's okay, you will be okay." Janet broke out a bottle of champagne for this memorable moment, making the final, but not last, toast to Tom.

It was time for Tom's rite of passage. I gave everyone their own bag of ashes and we took turns giving our final words, whispers and wishes to our love, brother and friend.

As I poured his ashes into the waters, I felt his aura release in a swirl that somehow surrounded us with hugs and "thank you's." I could feel his energy charge me. It was perfect.

The deeds were done. We all felt a patch of "better" in our hearts.

Chapter Thirty-Two

Keep Calm

Time was irrelevant...
Alone...

Dear Tom,

   I am in Florida again and I am sitting in this lovely Parisian café having breakfast with me, myself and you (in my dreams). This place, aptly named "Paris in Town Le Café," has you written all over it, from the fresh pâté in the case with gorgeous fluffy croissants to bottles of champagne and jars of cornichons on the shelves. We would buy one of each and have our picnic lunch for later today. Perfect, if only you were here. I do feel your presence and your wink to the pretty waitress with the delicious French accent. I can hear you speaking to her in French and seeing your charm ooze over her softly and sweetly.

   The music in the background and the decor is as if we were in a little café in Paris. We said no regrets, but that is one of mine—that you never went to Paris to have that cheese crepe that was on your bucket list. Someday, I will go and bring you with me and we will enjoy those crepes together. For today, this lovely slice of heaven will do.

Love you, darling.

DURING THE END OF TOM'S ILLNESS AND AFTER his death, I did not wear any jewelry; not earrings, not even a watch. Time was irrelevant to me and I really didn't care what I looked like. It became too much effort to think about what to wear and to put myself together. In the past, my outfits were color coordinated and put together, always with a different matching watch from my one hundred-plus watch collection. Or should I call it watch addiction?

One day, I had to go to a meeting and did not want to let them see me losing my grip. So, I decided to make myself presentable. I rummaged about in my closets and drawers, trying to find something to wear. I was lost in the memories of different clothes I had worn to places with Tom. I would never be able to do that again. I could wear them, but it would never be the same. It was too much. The clothes felt like they were smothering me with what will never be.

I had to go to his closet to touch his clothes to feel his breath on me and make him feel close to me.

My mind raced. *How am I going to go on? How will I pick something out of all these memories to carry me through this one day? It doesn't matter what I wear or what I look like. Who will care? Why do I care? Why is this so hard?*

I have been through the hardest thing in my life, but I can't even get dressed? This is not what Tom would want for me.

I knew this in my heart and I knew I had to take one step at a time, just like he would want me to. I felt my strength returning; my conviction to go forward in a positive way increased. It's like a bouncing ball. Sometimes you have to go down to the ground to bounce high again.

I went back to my closet and picked out a pair of white slacks, white top and beige jacket. I decided to start at the beginning of the color spectrum, since this was a new beginning. It felt right.

Simplifying life is one of the most satisfying efforts I have found. It is the euphoria after eating and drinking the most luscious, decadent five-course meal, but you ate only one long, slinky green bean. That sounds outrageously crazy and I'm not recommending only eating green beans; I'm illustrating how living with simplicity has the power to grow the inner peace of your life and happiness and give you a level of comfort that is life changing.

It started on its own with my desperate feelings of loss. I had lost Tom, and I wanted to lose everything else in my life except for what would connect me to him. I was still in that fog which kept me focusing on nothing and doing nothing.

I have never been a do-nothing kind of person and was innately perplexed at how my life just stopped cold with nothing left to it.

The only makeup I wore was a single line of slate gray eyeliner on my top lid to hide the puffiness of crying. This camouflage worked well and helped me to not feel naked.

I chose a pair of simple, silver, mini diamond starfish earrings that Tom and I had bought when we were in Key

West at "our jeweler" the weekend he proposed to me. They felt right on my ears and they gave me an energy and strength I didn't think I had. I knew that strength came from Tom helping to push me forward.

From that day on, I wore nothing but starfish earrings of every color and type I could find in my travels. Those tiny earrings were like my suit of armor and courage. I felt strong and pretty at the same time. This one choice freed me from decision making. I didn't have to think about what jewelry to wear anymore. A tiny corner of my life became bright and comfortable.

I treated myself to an Alex and Ani bracelet, one that depicts the Starfish as an energy sign. According to myth: "the starfish is a resilient creature that constantly regenerates, intuitively navigates the sea, and directly impacts its ecological community. An ancient name for the Virgin Mary, the Star of the Sea symbolizes guidance, intuition, and vigilance. Wear the Starfish for divine guided direction and a heightened sense of potential."

No wonder I felt better wearing starfish earrings; I was regenerating.

Color also simplified me. Since it was the beginning of summer, I could not imagine wearing black. I love wearing black in the winters of New England, since it makes you look so much slimmer and tends to keep you warmer. Black is, of course, the old-school dress of mourning. There is not much old-school in this girl, and I knew wearing black would make everything that much more depressing. I did not want to be disrespectful, but I needed to heed my inner conscience.

For my dad's funeral, I wore a black dress with bold white flowers and felt right wearing black out of respect and love for him.

But for Tom's celebration, I wore a cream dress with a multicolored, beachy crystal necklace that he would have loved. I can't remember what I wore to my nephew's service since everything was a blur at that point, but I know it was appropriate and right for me.

It takes effort to decide what to wear every day. I decided to whittle my wardrobe down to two colors: white and pink. White was perfect. It was my mummy cloak of honor, with the absence of color and the absence of doom and gloom. It made me feel alive instead of dead with all my loved ones.

Since I had those rose-colored glasses on, I also chose pink.

Life was so much easier. Everything and anything was either pink or white. Shoes, sandals, flip flops, panties, bras, pants, shorts, shirts, dresses, scarves, wallets, sunglasses, lipstick, pocketbook, computer case, wireless mouse, tablet, towels, sheets; all white or pink with or without bling. Or silver, which is a derivative of white.

Bling always helped to brighten any gloomy day. I could make a purchase decision in the shortest amount of time. I barely had to think about it. I felt safe with my monochrome, comforting colors surrounding me like hugs from heaven, making me feel special and loved. The evolvement of simplicity created a new stylish mummy with a little bit of color, bling, and inner peace to step into the real world.

"Keep Calm and Carry On." I think they made that slogan with me in mind. This is how I made it through life when death had chased us fast and fiercely. I refused to accept a death sentence. I refused to get upset about it and crazy with Tom or anyone else. There were times, truth be told, when I could let go of keeping calm, especially when a cocktail was involved. But, for the most part, I tried my best to stay calm and to just carry on with a positive attitude that we could beat this thing labeled ALS.

The slogan was created in England by the government, along with other uplifting messages, to boost morale during World War II. Most of the numerous posters were tossed into the trash when the war ended, but a few survived. No one knows who coined this phrase, but whoever did, I am thankful to them.

When I was diagnosed with breast cancer back in 2003, one of my coworkers asked someone at work if I realized that I had cancer and that I might die. He said he was concerned for me because I was so calm, happy and acting as if nothing was wrong.

In my mind, I had decided to carry on as if nothing was wrong with me so that nothing would change. In my mind, if I did all the treatments and knew in my heart that I would not die from breast cancer, then I would not. So, my life went on in a more positive way. I appreciated everything and every moment that I had on this earth. Negativity could eat away at what I had left, and I was not going to let that happen.

People tell me I am the calmest person they know. I'm not sure what it is, but I do feel calmer inside myself since Tom died.

I was crazed with trying to find a solution to the madness of his illness and keeping up with it all while maintaining my positive exterior of hope and upbeat feelings. If I could be up, he would stay up, too.

Now what? I will "Keep Calm and Carry On."

When it came to life and death decisions, there was no thinking involved, you just had to react and do what needed to be done, immediately. In the beginning of Tom's illness, the decisions related to doctors, hospitals, and medical options. In the middle, it was all about additional medical help, equipment and food changes needed to assist him and keep him comfortable. I tried to keep it fun and interesting for our adventure together.

Toward the end of Tom's life, the decisions became harder, the options fewer; and in the very end, there was only one decision to make: where to die. It is incredible to me that we never discussed this important decision. We covered everything else except this small detail. In retrospect, I think Tom did not know how his end would come, and he decided to leave it to chance, or me.

I also learned to appreciate and crave the sanctity of the amazing doctors and nurses who were truly there to help us manage these diseases. They were the true saviors in our world; they shone bright and led the way. They always kept calm and carried on with great fortitude, setting excellent examples. They helped me to become a better advocate.

Merriam-Webster says that an advocate is:

1. one who pleads the cause of another; specifically: one that pleads the cause of another before a tribunal or judicial court

2. one who defends or maintains a cause or proposal

3. one who supports or promotes the interests of another

Number three aptly describes what most advocates can do for a person who is ill. They can learn all there is to know about the illness and become their eyes and ears to help with crucial decisions on care and next steps. Many times, the patient is not in any position to understand the details or options that might be available, nor does he or she have the energy or desire to do this. Most of the time, they just prefer to hide under the covers and hope that it goes away.

I wish there was a course on how to be a good Medical Advocate. It's not an easy job and should come with real training.

My rose-colored glasses were an absolute necessity. If I didn't have them when I did the research that seemed hopeless for beating this disease, I would have hidden under those covers with Tom.

I was Tom's advocate, being his eyes and ears to understand the medical terminology and do the research. I learned everything I could about the possibilities of his diagnosis; from the variations of Lyme Disease to various central nervous system diseases, and the different forms of ALS. But more importantly, I helped him to make informed decisions that would frame his life.

It is a diligent, level-headed job, crucial to protect the patient from dealing with anything unsavory, upsetting or difficult. I wish I could have brought survival through the hell hand we were dealt, but I did the best I could to survive in other ways.

The testament to what I did is that several friends and family have asked me to be their advocate when and if they need one. The idea is complimentary and daunting at the same time.

People are not only dealing with illness but also insurance. Our insurance world is a tragedy. I had good insurance and could not imagine how someone would stay alive if they did not have reasonable insurance or an advocate.

The insurance world was exasperating! When Tom needed a critical, potentially lifesaving treatment of IVIG, it took us five months and fifty plus phone calls, letters and pleas of urgency to accomplish the task.

The medical profession is comprised of an assortment of characters who range from compassionate, warm, caring individuals to the coldest fish in the sea, who think they can be the tribunal of life and death. My wish is for the cold fish to get eaten by the sharks.

I also found miracle workers. These are the beautiful people who care about the patient and figure out how to make things happen quickly without delay. They make miracles happen every day. I see beautiful, glowing halos hovering over their heads. They are the ones that allow you to continue with the fight to beat this disease. They are the ones who make you smile and fill your heart with hope.

My hope carries on with the tiny things. Tiny things keep me going. Tiny things connect me to a feeling, a look, an ability to live again. It is the tiny things that allow me to put one foot in front of each other to stand as strong as I can be.

I know I will be stronger every day.

I know I can do this.

I know Tom will be with me, no matter what.

I know in my heart.

When I roll out of bed in the morning, Tom's smiling face greets me, to help me smile, too. Sometimes, I can see him winking at me.

I think about the bar of soap in the shower. A random thought that grounds me to the fact that here and there, I can touch my loved ones every day of my life. I just need to look at that bar of oatmeal soap in the shower, which was his favorite, and he touches me.

I look at a picture of my dad on the side of the fridge, while I'm making coffee in the morning, and I can see that twinkle in Dad's eye, just for me. My nephew comes to me in the form of black dragonflies, crows, or other wildlife, his signature way of dressing that touches me with love.

When I'm there with them someday, they will touch, hug and love me more than they do today. It is a beautiful thought. The tiny things fill me with hope that I can make it on my own.

Chapter Thirty-Three
Labor Day Weekend, 2014
The Last Day

I was incredibly happy.

IT WAS THE LAST DAY ON BLOCK ISLAND OF MY
four-day Labor Day weekend.

I woke early in the morning with the excitement of going
to take a picture of my heart on the beach. My friends were
going to join me, but after a long night, there were no tak-
ers. When I headed out, there were hardly any people in
the streets, just the same few runners and dog walkers.

As I walked past the National, something shiny caught
my eye on the sidewalk. A dime from Dad sat there gazing
up at me. It was like a remote microphone. I could hear
him saying, *You need to call your Mom to let her know you
are okay.*

Oh jeez, I forgot to call Mom. *Thank you, Dad, I will
call her after my walk, I love you.*

I love you, too. I put that dime in my pocket, which felt
warm and comfy, just like Dad.

When I cut through to the beach, I was surprised that
the ocean was flat, and the sea was out. There were hardly
any waves, but it was still beautiful, with a stark contrast of

baby blue skies and the ocean washing those silk stockings of sand. The day seemed brighter.

I thought how lucky I was to be here with my best friends; these people and this place could help heal me and my heart. I felt a tad better, like I could breathe a little easier.

I continued to walk to the same spot on Crescent Beach and sat down to have a talk with Tom. I told him how much I loved him and missed him. I told him that he was in my heart always, as I will always be with him. Our hearts were connected forever. I picked myself up and started to walk back, remembering that special heart he had given me when we arrived on the island. That's when I decided to give him a heart.

I formed a heart in the sand with the beautiful smooth, round or oblong rocks and stones that are always on Block Island beaches.

As soon as I finished laying them down, a wave came and took them all away! The tides had turned and came in with that undeniable force of nature.

I recreated the heart, using larger stones to make them stay longer, pushing them deep into the sand. The waves came. My heart held firm for a little bit, and then the waves started pulling the stones one at a time. I took pictures; it reminded me of our last three years and how eventual his passing was.

It was a little at a time; gentle, smooth and unexpected. I couldn't stay until my heart was all gone, because I couldn't bear to lose him again. I needed to leave before I got too emotional.

Just before I walked away, the ocean rolled up a small stone in front of the heart I had made. Oh, my God! It was amazing! It was perfectly shaped stone heart about the diameter of a quarter at the widest spread, light orange in color with gray running through like granite, flat on both sides, and about as thick as a cracker.

Tom was right there with me, sharing our hearts and our love. He was telling me how much he loved me and that he would always be there for me one way or another. I had proof that I could touch. I was incredibly happy. I don't question how these things happen; I know they are not coincidences. I embrace them wholeheartedly as living proof that I am connected to my loved ones and always will be. They help me to know that I am not alone and will never be alone. He is still very connected to me in so many amazing ways. He will never be forgotten.

Finding a new plateau in your mind is tricky business. Being here on Block Island has changed my way of thinking. This island and my friends have shown me how to relax and make the most of everything in the here and now.

I am extremely sad to leave this place of peace and connection. This island has cast a magical spell on me. I survived. I learned how to really smile again without feeling the ghosts of regret haunting me. I can laugh again without feeling guilty for the enormous loss. I feel more like a human being than I have in a long, long time. I have hope again.

I am still afraid of the future and what it will mean for me, but I feel now that my strength will carry me to where I am predestined to be, and who I will be. I guess that someday, somehow, I will feel like a normal person again, going about a normal life, whatever that is supposed to be.

How does anyone go through this loss and ever be whole, or anything close to normal again? The real question is whether I will have the mindset to pick myself up to live the fullest life I can without Tom by my side.

Can I overcome this deep, painful loss of my heart and soul? Can I ever feel again? Can I be strong again with a positive attitude?

I don't know if it's possible, but I will try and know that I will have a little help from my friends to bop on. This is what Tom wanted for me. I will share it with him every single day, and he will be with me. I can do this.

Epilogue
2016–2017

Paris

I'm just curious . . .

I TURNED ON MY COMPUTER ONE JUNE MORNING
and checked into Yahoo. An email popped onto my screen:
"Where will you be at the stroke of midnight on New Year's
Eve 2016? Find out here."

I don't know—where will I be, Tom?

I felt like I was in the Twilight Zone . . . there was a
greater power at work here to help me. I pushed the button
to find out, and although many destinations were displayed
in the ad, one jumped off the page: "New Year's Eve in Paris,
The City Experience."

I had promised Tom. Nothing else mattered.

I don't normally do group tours, but this one created an
inviting simplicity. I called the company and asked all the
right questions, trying to find something wrong. Nothing
was wrong. It was perfect. Paris, New Year's Eve, most of the
time by myself, but still some time with a handful of people.
Did I say *Paris*?

It was almost too good to be true. I could fulfill my
promise, get out of Dodge for this tough holiday for me,

and enjoy a new experience. I slept on it that night, didn't sleep much, dreamed about Tom and Paris, woke up and booked it first thing.

Six months flew by like a freight train on a mission. I was on that mission, too. My mission was to bring Tom's ashes to Paris, have that cheese crepe for him that was on his bucket list, and savor all the French savoir faire I could absorb. The agenda was short and sweet, just like our time together. Before I knew it, it was time to pack. I had purchased a small, screw top urn to transport the essence of his ashes to be packed with love in my suitcase.

People-watching is a favorite pastime of mine at airports. We are all part of the fabric of life rolled out into segments of colorful, entertaining cloth. There are those afraid of the person sitting next to them; and then the affable, open and friendly sort, those who crave a friendly face, word, or to share a story of their travels. I am mostly fortunate to meet the latter, and this trip did not disappoint.

As I settled into a packed bar, amongst two beautiful young women, I felt serendipity surround me. It did not take long for dialogue to follow the feeling.

"Don't order the soup. It's crap, salt pillars are growing in it." This girl was young, sassy and seemed to be well traveled.

"Thanks, I won't. I think I'll try the flatbread; I don't think they can kill that. Where are you traveling to?"

"Alingsås, Sweden. I am meeting friends I traveled in Asia with last year. It will be my only chance to see them this year, then on to Dublin with another friend."

"Wow, that sounds like a great trip. I love Dublin. My name is Jo Ann."

"Hi, my name is Meghan, where are you going?"

"Paris."

"Solo?"

"Yes, I'm really looking forward to it."

"Why are you going by yourself?"

Tough question to answer to a stranger, but why not? "I promised my husband, who passed away, that I would go to Paris for him and have the cheese crepe he wanted to have there."

"Oh, I'm so sorry."

"It's okay, I'm okay. He will be with me, I will not be alone."

"Jo Ann, I bet you will have an empty seat next to you on the plane, for him."

"Thank you, that would be nice."

The conversation continued about our stories, and then the gal next to us became intrigued and joined in. She was a comedian in London. They both wanted to know more about Tom and what happened. I told them I wrote a book and when it gets published, they can read it to learn the whole story. We exchanged information, became Facebook friends, and wished each other safe travel and good times.

The flight was uneventful, cold and long, but that seat next to me was empty for Tom to keep me company. A bright chilly day welcomed me to Paris, bidding me a warm *Bonjour!*

By day, the City of Light was a bustling, organized beauty of a place. The architecture saluted you with dress right dress authority, while the people walking, driving or riding bicycles marched in organized chaos. It was how it should be. Everyone had a purpose and a place. I wanted to be part of it.

I joined the forces on the street to explore and meld into the shuffle. It did not take long to come across a street vendor making crepes, which became my first bite in Paris. The gentleman made crepes as if he was the maestro for the New York Philharmonic Orchestra. The wooden T-shaped crepe spreader moved swiftly and deliberately over the crepe batter on the large round burner to make an expert, delightful caboose for savory or sweet delights to be added.

My request was simple: just cheese.

"Cheese and egg?"

"No, just cheese."

"Cheese and ham?"

"No, just *fromage, merci.*"

But it was not *just* cheese, it was gobs of shredded Gruyère cheese, added to this toasty lace tapestry of art, folded once then twice with the flick of a wrist, then pushed into a paper cone for me to walk away and eat. The aroma was decadent, the first bite was heaven.

I walked through the crowds of Parisians, devouring one small bite at a time, feeling like a tourist who had come home. Tom knew what he was talking about. This should be on everyone's bucket list.

I had expected to roam this gorgeous city alone, with Tom in my heart, to explore and let it talk to me in its own way, but fate had a different plan for me. I was fortunate to connect immediately with two wonderful women in our group who were also traveling solo. Kindred spirits, we joined forces immediately to become the three musketeers on this trip. Others in the group thought that Liliana, Victoria and I were lifelong friends.

Our merry band expanded to add more special folks, to settle into a rhythm of camaraderie. We typically met for our traditional European breakfast of fluffy warm croissants, meats, cheeses, creamy dreamy yogurt with fresh fruit, and French scrambled eggs and bacon. Then, in the evening, after a day of exploration, we would head back to the bar with our favorite bartender, Bruno, for a PC (Proper Cocktail, Tom).

One day dipped into the next, creating a masterpiece of art, history, friendship, fine food and drink (decadent Burgundy escargot and delicious dry Rose from Provence a highlight), and a tinge of contentment. For me, this mural could go on forever.

I was especially captured by the 18th *arrondissement* (neighborhood) of Montmartre, where we stayed. This was the artist's haven where the Impressionist period was borne. I saw where Edgar Degas lived, where Pablo Picasso painted his Blue Series of paintings, where Henri de Toulouse-Lautrec roamed and made his living.

As I sat at the bar of the Chat Noir (Black Cat Café) from 1881, probably where Toulouse-Lautrec sat one day, a feeling of melancholy came over me, wishing I could have been there with them, creating history.

One of my favorite artists is Toulouse-Lautrec who is among the best-known painters of the Post-Impressionist period, with Cézanne, Van Gogh and Gauguin. I walked in their footsteps, feeling like I needed to paint again, too. Tom always encouraged me to continue with my art, even though there was no time or ability to concentrate on it with all there was to do. I truly believe that he secretly knew how much Paris would affect me and make we want to pick up that paint brush again. Kudos to you, my love.

The group took off for Versailles one day, and I had my day to myself. I chose to roam around the streets of Montmartre, soaking up the vibe, shopping and inhaling the deliciousness around me. The streets were sparse, few people and cars, but the Parisians held court with their morning coffee and newspaper in the outdoor seating of the cafés lining the street.

The wide-open markets lined the edge of the streets. They had fresh fruits and vegetables, along with treasures from the seas, from tiny delectable clams to oysters of every size and color, to the freshest fish. I ate an entire meal with my eyes.

It was a green apple day; crisp, sweet and tart at the same time. The sun had taken a sabbatical, so my rose-colored glasses were perfect to catch every glimpse.

It was a good day to reflect on being in Paris, without Tom by my side but in my heart. I had finished writing my book, and I wondered what my future would bring.

Being in the heart of art pulled on those strings, as I remembered the simple joy of painting and creating something special; this gave me hope for the future. If only he could be here with me.

I walked into a boutique and, as soon as I did, the song "Unforgettable" started playing. I instantly thought that Tom was singing it to me. It was probably just a coincidence of walking in at the same time that the song started, but I felt he might be with me.

My next stop was a shop with a sidewalk display of colorful felt ponchos. I stepped inside to try one on. Immediately, I heard the first chords of the song, "Somewhere over the Rainbow" by Izzy Kamakawiwo'ole, and knew that Tom was right there with me, helping me try this poncho on, telling me how beautiful I looked in it.

The tears started streaming. *He is with me. How could I ever doubt that?*

My feet were stuck to the floor. I couldn't move if I wanted to. The clerk was concerned that I might be a crazy American she'd have to deal with, but she had other people to help, thankfully.

When the song ended, I paid for the poncho and turned to look back, just to see if he was there watching me behind my back. As I walked down the street, a couple of years of tears that had not fallen, dropped to the ground and mixed with the first rain drops of the day from somewhere over the rainbow. Perfect. The romance of Paris touched Tom and me.

And then there was New Year's Eve. This night was the reason for being here in Paris, besides my promise to Tom; but when it crept up, it took me by surprise. My emotions were not ready.

My emotions were tucked into bed like good little children should be. I didn't know if they would wake up or not and how they would be . . . sleepy little ones clinging with a hug of love, or loud cantankerous rabble-rousers screaming at the top of their lungs.

The day started out with the thrill of climbing the Eiffel Tower with endless views in every direction. Everything looked up. My spirits were high, thinking of the possibilities of a new year and how the energy of the city fed me like a queen. It seemed that anything was possible; just what would that be? I knew it was up to me.

The day spread out in front of us like a panoramic painting of Paris at its best with gorgeous views of the river, architecture, Parisians and panache at every corner. It was a myriad of color, shape, texture and thrill.

My new friend Liliana and I walked the painting eight miles back to our hotel from the Eiffel, savoring every corner of it.

I expected the evening to be the highlight of the trip and dressed accordingly in a black jumpsuit, large bling starfish earrings, and more bling around my neck.

The group received "New Year's Eve" tiaras for the women and hats for the men, along with noisemakers and whistles to celebrate that stroke of midnight. Our host started the merriment with a champagne toast and escargot for all in our group. It was festive and fun, the camaraderie of the group comforting.

This night was billed to be a view of all of Paris with fireworks, and the best view of the City of Light.

Unfortunately, it was not doable due to the gray weather and the threat of terrorists. So, we had to cancel the fireworks and blow out our candles. It became a lowlight of a night in a delightfully French historic café with a four-course meal that made your lips purr. We were in another life in another world just enjoying . . . Carpe diem.

Then it was almost midnight.

Those little darlings crept out of bed, covered my eyes and said "Boo." I could not imagine being here now, without Tom. I was in a boat of beautiful people thrilled to celebrate a new year, but I needed to bail out fast.

I excused myself, wrangled out of the thick of it and looked for a spot to call my own. There were none; every edge was filled to the brim. The only exit was to the bone-chilling cold outside, or the restrooms downstairs. Freezing was not an option . . . down the stairs I went. I could take refuge there.

"Where will you be at the stroke of midnight on this New Year's Eve?"

In the loo, with those sleepy little emotions hugging me and catching my tears. I heard the excitement of midnight upstairs, hugged myself and was glad to be alone.

This was the year for me. As I re-boarded the boat upstairs, the tears would not stop. Our wonderful host, Adoram, saw me. "Jo Ann are you all right?"

It was hard for me to talk. Adoram, being the most patient man I have met in a long time, gave me my time with grave concern.

"I'm fine, just having a moment. Happy New Year, Adoram." A hug and a kiss from a virtual stranger turned friend felt warm and fuzzy.

"I'm sorry, Jo Ann, can I get you something? Water, coffee, alcohol?"

Now he was talking my language. "Vodka on the rocks, please."

Adoram left my side and returned with the manager, who was French to the bone with a delicious accent, scarf tied around his neck and dark soulful eyes that captured your heart. "Madame, how can I help?"

"Do you have vodka?"

He made a puzzled face. "No."

"Do you have gin?"

A big broad smile answered my question. "*Oui, Madame!*"

"Lovely. Gin, rocks, lime if you have it, *s'il vous plaît.*"

Three seconds later, a tall frosty glass with my beverage of choice graced my hand. "*Merci, Monsieur.*"

The drink went down the hatch as a salute to the New Year, and the tears disappeared.

On the last day, four of us ventured to the Musée D'Orsay, where the major Impressionist paintings were on display. The delight of seeing the work of these great artists work was intoxicating. I hoped their mood, talent and expertise would rub off on me.

It was time for Tom's ashes to join the Seine River and be part of Paris. As we walked toward the Seine, I wished that the lock bridge was still intact. There was a tradition of lovers writing their names on a lock, fastening it to the famous Pont des Arts, and throwing the keys into the Seine, to lock their love for each other forever.

Recently, the locks were taken down, because they were too heavy for the bridge. But, my wish came true. As we walked along the Seine, we found that the bridge did exist. I couldn't believe my eyes, approaching this walking bridge, seeing locks on it, and someone selling locks. It was meant to be, just for me and a million other lovers that will visit Paris in the future. The vendor even had a bright pink lock that stood out in the crowd. I locked our love on that bridge, tossed the keys into the Seine along with some of Tom's ashes and felt that my mission was accomplished. I could go home now with total contentment.

We had a farewell dinner at the Chat Noir, soaking up more the artists' hearts and souls. It was a joyous occasion with new good friends who would stay part of my life. We had the added pleasure of a beautiful, sultry-voiced pianist crooning to us, the hum of the busy restaurant singing along in the background.

I asked our tour guide, who had lived in Paris for many years, a question that tugged at me. "Adoram, I have a question for you."

"Sure, Jo Ann, how can I help?"

"Do you know the song, 'Somewhere over the Rainbow?'"

"I think so, was that in *The Wizard of Oz*?"

"Yes, that's the one. Have you ever heard it played here in Paris?"

He looked at me as if I was asking a trick question. "No,

I cannot say that I have ever heard it played in Paris, on the air or anywhere. Why do you ask?"

"I'm just curious. Thank you so much Adoram, for everything." Confirmation of my love, Tom, in Paris with me.

As I took a taxi to my hotel across town, where I stayed for the last two nights, with a gorgeous view of the Eiffel Tower from my room, I thought I was the luckiest girl in the world. I didn't want the night to end, so I went into a little café on the corner by my hotel and ordered a nightcap. Lovely soft jazz in the background, sparkly soft lights, with me, myself and I, alone with my Tom.

The waiter brought my glass of port and a little dish of munchies. I nibbled on pretzels and sipped my wine, savoring Paris wrapped around me, watching lovers strolling down the street after midnight, arm in arm. I was happy for them having that love, just like me.

It was time to call it a night. One more nibble . . .what was left in the dish? Two cracker hearts, side by side.

Home sweet home. It's surreal to be home, but I want to still feel like I am in Paris, so I try to recreate the best

French scrambled eggs with lots of butter and cream. I grab my eggs, coffee and newspapers that have stacked up, and settle into the comfy couch for a morning read to catch up on what has been happening in my corner of the world.

I turn on Pandora, and the music fills the room . . . "Unforgettable." Yes, it was you in Paris, playing this song for me.

I love you too, baby.

Au Revoir,

Jo Ann

Afterword
ALS– Some Treatments for the Untreatable

A Brief Review
Amiram Katz, MD

AMYOTROPHIC LATERAL SCLEROSIS (ALS), ALSO known as Lou Gehrig's disease, is a rapidly progressive neurological disease that attacks the nerve cells that are responsible for controlling voluntary muscles. The disease belongs to a group of disorders known as motor neuron diseases which are characterized by the gradual degeneration and death of motor neurons (www.ninds.nih.gov/disorders/amyotrophiclateralsclerosis/details_ALS.htm)

The rate at which ALS progresses can vary from one person to another. Although the mean survival time with ALS is three to five years (50% of people), significant number of patient live five to ten or more years (10%). Symptoms can begin in the muscles of speech and swallowing; or in the hands, arms, legs or feet.

Progressive muscle weakness and paralysis are universally experienced (www.alsa.org. February 2011). Based on U.S. population studies, approximately 5,600 people in the U.S. are diagnosed with ALS each year (15 new cases a day). It is estimated that as many as 30,000 Americans have the disease at any given time. According to the ALS CARE Database, 60% of the people are men and 93% are Caucasian. Most people who develop ALS are between the ages of 40 and 60, but younger and older people can also develop the disease (Shaw PJ. Amyotrophic lateral sclerosis and other motor neuron diseases. IN: Goldman L, Schafer A, Eds. *Cecil Medicine*. 24th ed. Philadelphia, PA. Saunders Elsevier; 2011: chap 418).

ALS is a devastating disease. As a neurologist, you see your patients vanishing under your eyes without being able to cure them. The patients with ALS are many times the kindest people you'll ever meet. I always wondered why the kindest are getting the worst neurological illness, but would force myself not to try and look for answers to this question due to the bitter theophilosophical answers, e.g., reliving the story of Job (a trial of faith by God, without the happy ending), kindness is weakness, no good deed goes unpunished, etc.

When practicing neurology in a Lyme endemic state with no real therapeutic options for motor neuron disease, testing for and diagnosing and treating central nervous system Lyme (when present) is extremely important.

Any insult to the central nervous system which is already impaired by an existing condition would amplify the existing deficits significantly.

A patient with motor neuron disease who contracts Lyme disease, for which he is treated, might show significant improvement of the underlying condition due to the elimination of the additional insult. This might create an illusion of curing the underlying degenerative condition.

Another complicating factor in treating Lyme disease in patients with ALS, is that Rocephin and other beta lactam antibiotics can be helpful in this condition even when no infection is identified (Rothstein et al. β-lactam antibiotics offer neuroprotection by increasing glutamate transporter expression. *Nature.* 2005; 433:73–77).

Patients with ALS and Lyme disease were usually prescribed minocycline, which in addition to being an anti spirochetal agent, was believed to have neuroprotective properties (Yong et al. The Promise of Minocycline in Neurology. *Lancet neurology.* 2004; 3:744–750).

Unfortunately, a clinical trial with minocycline in patients with ALS, had to be terminated prematurely, due to accelerated mortality in the treatment group, when compared to the placebo control group. (Paul H Gordon, et al. Efficacy of minocycline in patients with amyotrophic lateral sclerosis: a phase III randomized trial. *Lancet Neurology* 2007; 6: 1045–53). My personal experience with it ALS patients, is that the tetracycline drugs, in general, might be associated with worsening of their clinical condition.

In a paper published 10 years ago (Harvey WT. Martz D. Motor neuron disease recovery associated with IV ceftriaxone and anti-Babesia therapy. *ActaNeurologicaScandinavica.* 115:129–131, 2007), the story of Dr. David Martz of Colorado Springs, CO, outlined a harrowing journey through ALS . . . and back. He was diagnosed in April of 2003 with this disease, and was bedridden when he learned, via a friend who sent him a newspaper clipping, that it was possible he really contracted Lyme disease. Dr. Martz began using antibiotics to treat his ALS, and is now fully recovered and back at work treating ALS and Chronic

Lyme Disease sufferers in a private practice in Colorado Springs.

A multi center clinical trial, placebo controlled, assessed the role of ceftriaxone in ALS patients following the promising results of Rothstein (see above) in the mouse model of ALS. The results of phase II of the study (safety) were promising, but phase III (efficacy) didn't find statistically significant differences in the ALS scale between the placebo and the ceftriaxone group (Cudkovicz, ME et al. Safety and efficacy of ceftriaxone for ALS: a multiphase, randomized, placebo controlled trial. *Lancet Neurology*, 2014; 13:1083–1091).The study designers were not familiar with long term IV ceftriaxone administration and the protocol used double the standard daily dose of the drug and didn't follow liver functions and white blood count weekly, but only once a month. They also didn't check for a common complication of ceftriax one therapy—gall stones. The patients with side effects were not eliminated from the study, which most likely skewed the results and contributed to the disappointing conclusion the ceftriaxone treatment doesn't help patients with ALS.

No cure has yet been found for ALS. However, the FDA approved the first drug for treating this disease, riluzole (Rilutek), in 1995. Riluzole has shown to prolong survival by several months, mainly in those patients with difficulty swallowing.

Last development in treating ALS was the approval of a new drug by the FDA in May of 2017. The drug—Radicava (edaravone) has been around for some time and was used to treat a variety of acute neurological conditions by reducing the associated oxidative damage with some success. In a clinical trial completed in Japan, after 24 weeks, the treatment group showed a 5 point less decline on the ALSFS-R (ALS functional scale) compared to the control group.

Recent promises in treating ALS appear to related to stem cells therapy. A phase 1&2 multicenter trial where spinal cord derived homologous (human) neuronal stem cells were injected directly into the anterior horn of the spinal cord (site of the dying motor neurons) in the cervical and lumbar regions was completed in 2015. A total of 15 patients were studied and showed no significant clinical improvement. There were infrequent complications. In an editorial in the journal Neurology (2016; 87:392–400) it was recommended to extend the number of patients enrolled and deliver larger quantities of stem cells. In patients who died later on from the disease, autopsies showed no evidence of stem cells proliferation in the injected sites.

The Israeli company Brain Storm sponsored an American multi centered, placebo controlled, autologous (patient's own) Bone Marraw Derived Stem Cells (BMDSC) injected into the subarachnoid space via a spinal tap (ClinicalTrials.gov Identifier: NCT02017912). The BMDSC underwent a proprietary treatment prior to implantation, allegedly inducing the formation of a variety nerve growth factors, including neuronal. Although the study was completed in 2016, The results were not yet published.

The role of memantine—Namenda (Wang and Zhang. Memantine prolongs survival in an amyotrophic lateral sclerosis mouse model. *European Journal of neuroscience.* 2005; 22:2378–80) in ALS is interesting and this agent should be used due to its antiglutamate neuro-protective properties.

The fact that no cure is yet found, doesn't mean that no help can be offered to ALS patients. A variety of supportive devices, respiratory and communication aids are available to the patients. An optimistic approach, sometimes accompanied by the pharmacologic aid of anti depressants can make a big difference in the quality of the short remaining life of many of the patients.

Information for Further Research

Bulbar Amyotrophic Lateral Sclerosis (Bulbar ALS)
https://als.ca/wp-content/uploads/2017/02/BulbarALS
-English.pdf

Electromyography (EMG)
https://www.mayoclinic.org/tests-procedures/emg/about/
pac-20393913

ALS vs. Lyme Disease
http://alsn.mda.org/article/als-doesn%E2%80%99t
-masquerade-lyme-disease-experts-say
https://www.huffingtonpost.com/david-michael-conner/
man-diagnosed-with-als-di_b_8891262.html

Lyme Disease Association, Inc. (LDA)
www.lymenet.org
https://www.lymediseaseassociation.org/doctors

Gout
https://en.wikipedia.org/wiki/Gout

Lyme Literate Doctors (LLMD)
http://mylymediseasetreatment.com/

http://mylymediseasetreatment.com/lyme-disease
-general/how-to-find-a-lyme-literate-doctor-llmd
-in-your-area/

Hemochromatosis
https://www.hemochromatosis.org/#overview

Chronic Lymphocytic Leukemia
https://www.cancer.org/cancer/chronic-lymphocytic
-leukemia/about/what-is-cll.html

The Ice Bucket Challenge
https://www.cnn.com/2015/07/15/health/one-summer-
after-the-als-ice-bucket-challenge/index.html

Healing Touch
https://www.healingtouchprogram.com/about/
what-is-healing-touch

ALS Association
www.alsa.org

Lyme Disease
www.lymedisease.org

Centers for Disease Control and Prevention
https://www.cdc.gov/lyme/index.html

American Lyme Disease Foundation
www.aldf.com

Lyme Disease Association
https://www.lymediseaseassociation.org

Lyme Disease Challenge
http://lymediseasechallenge.org/

Lyme Disease Research Database
www.lyme-disease-research-database.com

International Lyme and Associated Diseases Society
www.ilads.org

Visiting Nurse Associations of America
www.vnaa.org

National Hospice and Palliative Care Organization
www.nhpco.org

Idiopathic Thrombocytopenic Purpura (ITP)
https://www.mayoclinic.org/diseases-conditions/
idiopathic-thrombocytopenic-purpura/symptoms-causes/
syc-20352325

Oligoclonal Bands and Demyelinating Disease
https://en.wikipedia.org/wiki/Oligoclonal_band

Hemochromatosis
www.hemochromatosis.org/#overview

Intravenous immunoglobulin (IVIG)
http://www.ncbi.nlm.nih.gov/pmc/articles/PMC1809480

Multifocal Motor Neuropothy (MMN)
https://www.gbs-cidp.org/variants/multifocal-motor
-neuropathy/multifocal-motor-neuropathy-mmn
-progress-challenges/

Acknowledgments

To my dear Tom, who created the story to be written.

My gratitude stems from the love, compassion, and support from all of the people who made a difference in my life and the end of life for Tom. These are a special breed that make a difference, give you hope, and warm your soul. The list is long, with special mention to friends, family, coworkers, doctors, nurses, Danbury Hospital, Lyme Research Center, Hospice, and ALS Association staff.

This book would not have been possible without the ongoing support of my friends, family, and cowriters. It is amazing how they put up with me through the writing and did not let it be known that they were bored with my ongoing saga. Special thanks to my amazing editors, Barbara Ellis and MaryAnne Hafen who saw my vision and helped me to find the finish line, with "no sleep edits" through the night.

The effort to make a life the best it could be for as long as possible was won by all.

Thank you.

Message from the Author

Dear Reader,

Thank you for being part of my journey. I started writing so I would not forget anything about our short life together. As I wrote, I realized that these words and memories were helping me to cope and have hope again for the future. I continued to publish my story to try to help others going through similar situations.

Hopefully, I have helped you to have rose-colored glasses too.

I would be grateful if you could please take a moment to post a short review of *Rose-Colored Glasses* on Amazon and Goodreads. Feedback is what smiles are made of. Thank you in advance.

Hearing from my readers and book clubs who have selected my book to read would be especially heartwarming.

Jo Ann Simon

Contact me:
Website: www.joann-simon.com
Facebook: joannsimonauthor
Twitter: @forgetmenotjosi
Instagram: forgetmenotjosi

Book Club
Discussion Questions

What factors led the author to finally let her husband go? What considerations go into making the decision to let someone go?

To what extent can writing serve as therapy?

How can we provide support to people dealing with terminal illness?

The author describes feelings of peace when hearing certain sentimental songs. What connection does music have to emotions?

What are the advantages and dangers of seeing the world through rose-colored glasses? What other attitudes do people take on when confronting difficult situations?

What is the value of hearing individual stories when dealing with fighting a disease or medical condition on a large scale?

How do environment and color, in particular, factor into our outlook on life?

What is the value of connecting coincidence more intimately to our lives?

As stated in several places throughout the book and in the Message from the Author, one of the reasons the author wrote the book was to remember everything that happened. Is there a price we pay for remembering? What is to be gained?

Will the author's cheery outlook allow her to find a new love? Can she believe the cycle of Love, Loss, and Hope is a continuous loop?

Can you identify a time when you have chosen to trust in great love, donning rose-colored glasses even when the odds were against you?